Swan Lessons

A Bereaved
Mother's
Story of
Courage
and
Discovery

Joyce A. Harvey

Robert D. Reed Publishers

Robert D. Reed Publishers • Bandon, OR

Robert D. Reed Publishers
P.O. Box 1992
Bandon, OR 97411
Phone: 541-347-9882; Fax: -9883
E-mail: 4bobreed@msn.com
Website: www.rdrpublishers.com

Editor: Cleone Reed
Front Cover Artist: Cliff Upp
Cover Designer: Cleone Reed
Book Designer: Amy Cole

Permission to quote from *Renascence* and *The Poet and His Book* by
Edna St. Vincent Millay, courtesy of the Millay Society (millay.org).

Soft Cover: 978-1-944297-90-9
EBook: 978-1-944297-91-6
Library of Congress Control Number: 2021930066

Designed and Formatted in the United States of America

*The events described in this book are based on the author's recollections
of how they occurred at the time. Other than family, names have been
changed for most of the people mentioned out of respect for their privacy.*

Dedication

For my daughter Jennifer,
whose short life continues to inspire me
and
For my soul sister, Annie,
who recognized the true nature of my soul,
and has been an unconditional source of love and support.

Contents

Acknowledgments

I want to thank all my friends and colleagues who read the manuscript and gave me feedback. (You know who you are.) And thanks to my unofficial Project Manager, all things non-literary, Dawn Hardy, another soul sister.

A special thank you to my publisher Robert Reed Publishers, who recognized the merits of the book and the need for it to be published at this point in time.

Thank you to my editor Cleone Reed, who was a delight to work with, and to Cliff Upp who captured my vision for the cover art.

And I thank my family for their enduring love.

Introduction

I wrote *Swan Lessons* in the first few years following the death of my daughter Jennifer. It was not an easy book to write. It was truly a labor of love. I didn't write the chapters in order. When I finally got the courage to write the first chapter, I metaphorically strapped myself to my chair because I knew if I paused, I would never complete it. So, I wrote with tears streaming down my face, and when I finished, I collapsed face down on the couch for three days and sobbed.

Throughout the years, I would edit and re-edit the manuscript, polishing it for the time, if and when, it was right to have it published. Then 2020 and COVID hit, and hundreds of thousands of people lost loved ones and were left grieving.

It was time.

It is not easy to let my personal life and the life of my deceased daughter become public. But this is my gift to you, the reader. If you've lost someone, perhaps you will find healing and peace in the following pages. Perhaps you will become more aware. I could tell you your deceased loved one is always with you, but if you are like me, you'll need to discover that for yourself. Maybe you will find your answers in the pages of *Swan Lessons*.

A loss or serious emotional traumatic event seems to be followed by a struggle to find meaning in death and suffering. "Traditional" ways of coping with grief don't seem to work in today's complicated world. Those suffering may become discouraged with the responses provided by clergy and the professional community ... perhaps because there is more to uncover.

When one loses a child, part of the healing process may be to explore spiritual issues, particularly questions of the *viability* of the spirit or soul of the deceased. As I write in *Swan Lessons* when addressing this very issue, "Even if a person never had a spiritual thought or question before the death of her child, she does afterward. I don't know how to process this trauma without discussing the spiritual aspects. It would be like trying to describe the sinking of a ship without mentioning the water." The readers are allowed to comfortably bring their own spiritual beliefs, and perhaps expand upon them, as they journey through the book.

In a culture that only wants to "feel good," people who have experienced trauma are desperately reaching out for something that acknowledges the tremendous pain they feel, and yet, at the same time brings hope. They want to read about someone who has survived what they are attempting to survive. When they discover others with similar experiences and feelings, they breathe a sigh of relief and the healing journey begins.

Dean Ornish wrote in his book, *Love and Survival*: "For me, the most interesting books are ones in which the writer recreates his path for the reader, rather than acting like a guru coming down from the mountain to deliver a message. I usually find that the process of discovery is more interesting than the answers." It is in this vein *Swan Lessons* was written.

The Beginning of the End

For something in you dies when you bear the unbearable.

And it is only in that dark night of the soul

that you are prepared to see as God sees

and to love as God loves.

~ Ram Dass, "A Letter to Rachel"

"Mom, they are out to destroy my military career!" My daughter, Jennifer, called sounding very distraught. It was the fall of 1995. She was serving in the Marine Corps, stationed at Headquarters, Marine Corps (HMC) in Arlington, Virginia.

"I've worked too hard to get this far, and I'm not going to let them do that."

"How do you know that's what's happening?" I asked.

"Dick told me."

"Do you think Dick is telling the truth?"

"Yes," she said. "He wouldn't lie about that."

Dick and Jen worked in the same office and, as it turned out, he had been telling the truth. However, he didn't tell her the whole story. Not only was he a witness to the defamation of her name, he was a part of it. Jen wasn't aware of that at the time.

My thoughts flashed to the previous Thanksgiving, when she brought Dick home with her. I experienced all kinds of negative intuitive alarms when I first met him. I couldn't sleep the entire time he was in my house. I later told a friend Dick made my skin crawl. It wasn't necessarily anything he said or did. It was more like a sixth sense calling out to me.

When they first met, Dick told Jen he was divorcing his wife, who was living in California with their young daughter. He even flashed the divorce papers, he but failed to show her they weren't signed. Jennifer later learned Dick also had a girlfriend in Alabama, who he promised he wouldn't see anymore. He never kept that promise.

All of this began to unfold as their relationship progressed. Unfortunately, Jennifer was in love with him. She seemed determined to help him with his personal problems, especially with respect to his child. She encouraged him to keep in contact with his daughter, because she thought that's what a father should do.

Dick treated Jennifer poorly. He drank heavily and they often fought. In December of 1994, they decided to stop seeing each other. He was on his way to visit his daughter in California, which also meant he would be seeing his wife. Jen thought it would be best not to talk with him outside of work, since he was still legally married. Even though she made that decision intellectually, she was grieving the loss of the relationship.

I recently separated from my second husband, Tom, who was living in Houston, Texas. I moved back to my roots and was living in a little town in Michigan, close to the Ohio border, near Toledo.

Jen came home for the Christmas holidays. She requested a temporary assignment to work in the Toledo Marine recruiter's office for a month, so she could be at home longer. We were both happy to hear her request was granted. When she arrived home, however, she was moody and sullen.

The day after she arrived, I took her shopping, hoping it would help elevate her spirits. We wanted to find a gift for her stepbrother, Ben, who is Tom's son. He would be in town to spend Christmas with his mother, who also lived in Toledo, and planned to see Jen and me as well.

Ben was eight years old when I married his father; Jennifer was eleven. Her father, Russ, and I divorced when she was still a baby. Our backgrounds were so different and our futures were looking even more disparate. For example, I loved good conversation and that wasn't Russ's strong suit.

Maternity leave was difficult for me in some ways. Prior to the leave, I was teaching critical care nursing and I was used to interacting with others. After Jennifer was born, I looked forward to Russ's return home from work every day so I would have someone to talk with. I remember specifically the day that was the "last straw" for me. Jennifer, in all of her wondrous three weeks of age, did something I thought was magnificent. Maybe she smiled that day.

Without much of a greeting, Russ came home from work, picked up the newspaper, sat down, and began to read. I excitedly said, "Russ, guess what Jennifer did today?"

He lowered the paper and said to me, "Do you mind? I am reading the newspaper."

That was it for me. In retrospect, I think I was experiencing post-partum depression, although I had felt the voids in our marriage for some time. I'm sure Russ must have felt them as well.

Within weeks I moved out with Jennifer. It was not an easy move. It pained me deeply to hurt Russ in this way. My depression only worsened. And although it was not easy being a single parent, it was the right decision in the end. The marriage would not have lasted. By the time Jennifer was walking and talking, Russ found a new love and they are together to this day.

Russ and I retained an amicable relationship, not only for Jennifer, but because we genuinely liked each other. He remained close to my family as well, especially my brother, Patrick. Russ was a pallbearer for my father's funeral in 1985.

Ben spent a great deal of time with Tom, Jen and me, and he eventually came to live with us when he was fourteen. He and Jen were only two years apart and were very close. They always referred to each other as brother and sister—never stepbrother or stepsister. Likewise, I usually referred to Ben as my son. He's bright and sensitive like Jen. They had much in common.

Even though I treated Ben like a son, Tom never accepted Jennifer. It was as if he competed with her for my attention and saw her as an obstacle to his spending time with me. He never warmed up to her or showed her affection. Being a very sensitive child, she picked up on his attitude and they frequently butted heads. The atmosphere in our house was tense, which became worse as Jen grew into her teens.

In 1993 the four of us moved from Toledo to Houston, where Tom accepted a position as a clinical psychologist. The change of location didn't do anything to soften his attitude toward Jennifer. After seven years of marriage he still couldn't find room in his heart for my only child. Ten months after we moved to Texas, Jen and Tom had an altercation. Tom ordered her out of the house and told her she needed to live somewhere else. Jen was only seventeen. I told Tom that Jen and I were **both** going to live somewhere else. That was the final blow and we ended our marriage.

Jen entered the Marine Corps as soon as she was eighteen and I moved to Michigan. Ben stayed in Texas with his father but visited frequently with his mother in Toledo, as he would again in a few days.

As Jennifer and I walked through the various stores looking for Ben's gift, Jen asked, "When will Ben be in town?"

"On the twenty-fifth. I'd like to have his gift wrapped and ready when he arrives."

Jennifer did not appear to be enjoying the shopping and confirmed my assessment when she said, "Mom, I'm tired. Can we go home after we find something for Ben?"

We bought Ben's gift and left.

When Ben arrived a few days later, he seemed pleased to see us. Jen and I had missed him. He was an important part of our lives. He liked the sweater we chose for him. He gave me a pen in a stand, which was in the shape of Texas and decorated with bluebonnets, the state flower. Jen enjoyed the Alan Jackson Christmas CD Ben gave her.

The CD had special meaning. When we first moved to Texas, we entered a contest and won two tickets to Alan Jackson's performance at the Houston rodeo. Jen had just met Tristin, a handsome young man living in our neighborhood. She wanted to get to know him better and thought an invitation to the rodeo might be a good opportunity. Unfortunately, the concert was sold out.

Ben offered his ticket to Tristin. He knew Jen was saddened by the move and was struggling to meet new friends. It was one of Ben's most selfless acts. I was so proud of him. It was the first time Jen truly smiled since our move to Texas.

But she wasn't smiling now—even though she was home for the holidays. When Jen and I spent Christmas Eve with my family—my mother, brothers, and sisters—Jen sat alone moping and resisted any attempts to bring her into the activities. She was difficult to be around. At that point in time, I didn't recognize how depressed she was. She just seemed agitated and withdrawn.

We joined my family for dinner one evening in a restaurant. A few of my sisters liked to pick on me. Someone made a derogatory comment about me and she agreed. It's like there was peer pressure for her to agree, but for some reason it struck me wrong. I guess I expected her not to agree. I reacted with anger and irritability. I should have directed my anger at my sister who made the comment, but instead, I was angry with Jen.

The next day I wrote her a letter, which I have always regretted. I basically told her if she couldn't show respect for me, she wasn't welcome in my home.

That harsh statement was totally out of character for me with respect to Jen. With all the trials and tribulations she and I'd been through, I never reacted like this before. In fact, at one point, Tom complimented the patience and understanding I seemed to have with Jen as she was going through the turbulence of adolescence.

I guess what triggered this letter was I was tired of being the brunt of her anger, which seemed to have begun when I married Tom eight years prior. Jen and I had been living alone for almost eleven years before Tom and I married. We had a wonderful relationship, and she had become accustomed to having me all to herself. She didn't like sharing me, and she didn't like Tom.

He and I were now divorced, and it was time for this behavior to cease. I'd been living alone for the past nine months without the constant tension that existed between Tom, Jen and me, and I didn't want to go back to that. I'd never been as tough with her as I was in this letter. I picked a lousy time.

After I wrote the letter and placed it on her bed, I had an uneasy feeling I should retrieve it and wait to discuss the issue when we could talk face to face. But Jen could be so elusive, always disappearing if she sensed a serious conversation was about to happen. Every aspect of my being was shouting for me to retrieve that letter, but I ignored the intuitive messages.

When I came home from work the next day, Jen and her things were gone. I felt awful. I immediately called her at the recruiter's office.

"Jen, I didn't want you to move out. All I am asking you is to show respect toward me. Please come back home so we can talk."

"I don't want to talk about this right now," she replied and ended the conversation.

I sent her roses at work to let her know how sorry I was about the way I handled the issue. I planned to send them even before I wrote the letter, just to cheer her up. I told her on the card how much I loved her.

She did not come back home during her stay. She spent the rest of the week with my sister, Diane, who was like a second mother to Jen. During the time Jen and I lived alone, Diane stayed with her on the few occasions I traveled. They were very close.

Jen and I eventually got together a few days later to discuss what had happened. Diane acted as the referee, helping each of us to be heard.

The conversation was strained and difficult, but I think in the end, we both felt like we understood the other's point of view. Even so, I still didn't realize how depressed she was. She just seemed so angry and difficult to get along with.

She had a few more weeks left with her assignment as a recruiter's assistant, but she didn't like that type of work. She missed her job at HMC, where she was an administrative clerk. I also think she missed seeing Dick. She decided to return to Virginia earlier than planned. Our spat probably didn't help matters, even though we appeared to have reconciled our differences.

I warned her to be careful with Dick. He was due back from California. "Don't lose sight of the fact he just spent time with his wife. Keep that in perspective," I cautioned her.

When Jen returned to HMC, she had a new supervisor, NCOIC (Non-Commissioned Officer in Charge) Sgt. Wesson. Jen called me sounding frustrated and said, "My new Sergeant is married and he asked me out. I told him, 'No! You're married.' That's just what I need, Mom! To get involved with another married man."

Wesson obviously felt rebuffed. He began criticizing her work, a stark contrast to her other superiors who frequently praised her with verbal and written citations. "Mom, I even went into the office on my own time to do some of the work, hoping to please him. But he still criticizes me. I came into the office this morning and my top two desk drawers were sitting on my desk. My boxes were stacked up as well. Sgt. Wesson said to me, 'All this stuff has to go.'

"I asked him why and he told me I didn't need it. He said I could have two pictures of my family, but that was all I was allowed to display. He said the rest was not necessary. I told him I understood it wasn't necessary, but it wasn't hurting anyone.

"He said, 'I say it isn't necessary.'

"That was the end of the discussion. I was forced to remove all personal items from my desk except the picture of you and one of Dad."

Jennifer told me of incidents where Wesson would humiliate, degrade, and embarrass her publicly, sometimes to the point where she was reduced to tears. If she did cry, he would make her sit at her desk where she was highly visible. He wouldn't allow her to go to the restroom to fix her makeup.

Jen did not break down easily. In one of her letters from boot camp, she told me how her drill instructor repeatedly held her up as an example to the rest of the platoon of someone who was not weak. That was part of the reason she was chosen as the platoon Honor Graduate. The recipient of this award is one who "demonstrates a high degree of discipline, proficiency, bearing, and physical fitness."

Jen also graduated at the top of her MOS (Military Occupation Specialty) school for administration and personnel. She was meritoriously promoted to Private First Class upon graduation from boot camp, and then promoted to Lance Corporal upon graduation from MOS school. She was up for promotion to Corporal in April.

At Jen's graduation from boot camp, her senior drill instructor said to her father and me, "I have never been as impressed with a young Marine as I am with Pfc. Merrihew. I anticipate she will be a Sergeant within two years."

Wesson's superior officer, Staff Sgt. Sweeney, told him to "lay off" Jen, that she was a top-notch Marine. Sweeney frequently reminded Wesson that Jen was an Honor Graduate as well as top of her MOS school. Those reminders only seemed to make things worse with Wesson.

In addition to feeling the sting of being rebuffed, I think Wesson was envious of Jen. She was beautiful, bright, sharp, and quick. She had great leadership skills and displayed initiative. Someone like Jen might easily intimidate anyone not confident in his or her own abilities.

Jen had the opportunity to play on the National Marine Corps Volleyball team, but Wesson would not give his permission. Jen loved volleyball and played all through high school. I was very disturbed when I heard her request was denied. I felt certain playing on the team would have boosted her spirits.

The situation continued to deteriorate between both Dick and Jen, and Sgt. Wesson and Jen. I bought an airline ticket for Jen and brought her home for a weekend in March.

We sat at the kitchen table and talked about dealing with a personality like Wesson's. I had made a transition from teaching critical care nursing to teaching sales and management courses as an independent contractor.

"Jen, I teach a course on identifying basic social styles—ways people typically interact with their environment and with society. There are four basic styles, and once you know which type you're dealing with, you know how to interact more effectively. Do you want to see what style Wesson is?"

Jen was very interested, so I brought out a copy of the profile. I explained, "There are four sets of adjectives in each row. Rank each word in the row, giving a four to the word which best describes Wesson, a one to the word that least describes him, and so on."

She filled out a profile on Wesson and one for herself. He fell into the *analytical* and *driver* profile. "Both of this guy's styles are task oriented and not people oriented," I told Jen. "You have one task square and one people square. The best way to deal with someone of this profile is to be organized; don't be too casual; provide solid facts and don't question his authority. Try not to take his brusque manner personally. I know he's unfairly picking on you, but try not to be so sensitive about it." That was a tall order for someone as sensitive and conscientious as Jennifer.

We talked several hours. Jen even watched the films that were part of the course. I could see she was tired, so I suggested she take the training materials with her and continue to review them. She lay on the floor and asked me to give her a back rub, which I did. We had some good conversations over the weekend, and her anger toward me seemed to be gone.

I hated to drop her off at the airport when it was time for her to return to Virginia. I felt like I was sending her back into a lion's den. I just didn't know what I could do to help.

She was becoming more and more depressed working in the same office with both Dick and Wesson. Dick eventually made the decision to bring his wife and daughter to live with him on the base in an effort to salvage the marriage. Jen said he wanted to spend more time with his daughter.

When Jen tried to date other men, Dick would show up intoxicated at places she frequented, like the base club. He was obnoxious toward her and any man she might be talking with, even though his wife was now living with him. Jen had to face both Dick and Wesson every day at work, and it was taking its toll.

She filled out a formal request to be transferred to another base, but the request was denied. She again attempted to get some help by talking with Wesson's superior. Sweeny was appalled by what he heard. Once again, he told Wesson that Jen was a good Marine, and to stop picking on her. But the harassment continued.

In July of 1995, Jen came home for my sister Bobbi's wedding. I was in the bridal party, and on the day of the wedding, I had an appointment to get my nails done. I asked Jen if she wanted to get her nails done as well—my treat. She accepted.

She drove us over to the salon, and on the way, I happened to glance at her arms. It was the first time in a while I had seen her in a short-sleeved shirt. My stomach sank when I saw what looked like a scar on her left arm. "Jenny, what happened to your arm?" I asked her in a quivering voice.

"Nothing," she snapped. "I burned myself on an iron."

"Oh, Jenny … " I responded trembling. She knew I didn't buy her explanation.

"It was a long time ago and it's over now." She slammed the door on any further conversation.

The scar looked as if her arm had been cut. I was sick. In hindsight I realized we should have turned the car around, skipped the nail appointment, and gone home to talk. There wouldn't have been another opportunity to do so. Immediately after the appointment, we had to finish dressing and be on our way.

We were both unusually quiet at the salon. As the hairdresser worked with my hair, she suggested a sprig of baby's breath would look nice. Jen quickly volunteered to get some. She returned shortly with the delicate, white flowers. She looked deeply into my eyes and handed them to me as if they were a peace offering. Her beautiful, but sad brown eyes seemed to be saying, "I'm so sorry, Mom."

A friend of Jen's from the Marine base had driven with her to be her date for the wedding. He was waiting for us at home. Once we got back to the house, we were never alone again.

On a day that should have been joyous and fun, my heart was heavy. I suspected my daughter had attempted suicide, and I didn't know why or when.

Jen wore a white dress I loaned her. We wore the same clothing and shoe size (talk about sole/soul mates) and it was easy for us to share our wardrobe. She looked so beautiful with her dark hair, brown eyes, and tanned skin contrasting the white of the dress.

The last time Joyce and Jennifer were together

At the end of the ceremony, family pictures were taken. I am so glad we did. It was the last family picture she would ever be in.

At the reception, Jen sang a solo: "The Greatest Love of All." As I listened to her sing the words, "Learning to love yourself is the greatest gift of all," I choked back tears. Did she understand what she was singing? Did she believe it? Was there a special reason she picked that song? "No matter what they take from me, they can't take away my dignity .... "

She seemed to have a good time that evening; and she, her friend, and I drove home together. The next day, when she was preparing to leave, I held her. With tears streaming down my face I said, "Jen, if you are ever in that much pain again, please don't shut me out."

"I won't, Mom," she said softly.

Shortly after her return to the base at the end of July, Jen finally had an opportunity to get out of the office situation she found so difficult. Military police from the Marine Corps base are responsible for security at the Naval Command Post in the Pentagon. They were short security personnel, and Jennifer was temporarily assigned to protect this post. When she told me she would be carrying a weapon, I felt the strangest sensation in the pit of my stomach—as if it had dropped to the ground.

In boot camp, she achieved *Expert Shooter* status for rifle range ability, which is the top category one can achieve. In addition, she attained the highest shooting score in her platoon, for which she received the *Marksmanship Award*. On paper it appeared she was qualified to carry a gun.

Jennifer enjoyed her work at the Pentagon, and those working with her verbalized their appreciation of her dedication, positive attitude, and enthusiasm. She received numerous compliments from superior officers.

She was only there on a temporary assignment and would eventually be required to resume her previous position. She didn't want to go back. As her return to HMC loomed closer, she expressed to the supervisors in the military police her desire to remain in the security position. They wanted to keep her as strongly as she wanted to stay. But her superiors at HMC insisted she return to her position as administrative clerk.

On the phone one evening, during the second week of September, we discussed her dread of returning to HMC. "I'm not going back!" she stated emphatically.

I wasn't sure exactly what she meant, since it sounded to me as if she didn't have a choice.

She called me a few days later. "Mom, am I still on your medical insurance policy?"

"No, why are you asking?" Following the divorce, I had to buy my own insurance and Jen was covered by the military.

"I think I'm depressed and I need to see a psychologist. I'm having trouble sleeping. I've been seeing a counselor on the base, but my counseling records would be accessible to my superiors if they requested them.

I want to see a civilian psychologist for reasons of confidentiality. Will you help me find one?"

"Yes, I will, and I'll see what I can do to add you to my policy. In the meantime, don't worry about the money. I'll help you with your doctor bills. Just concentrate on getting better."

I called Tom to see if he knew any therapists in the Arlington area, or if he had a directory of psychologists who were accredited by the American Psychological Association. Ben, who was seventeen at the time, answered the phone. We chatted for a few minutes and he asked, "How's Jen doing?"

"Not very well at this point. She's having some problems at work and she's very sad right now. She could use a cheer-up call from you."

When Tom got on the phone it was clear he was not pleased to hear from me. He remarried, and perhaps his wife didn't appreciate my calling. I asked him if he could recommend anyone for Jen, and he said he didn't know of anyone in that area. I remembered meeting a colleague of Tom's who now lived in Virginia. I asked Tom if he would give me this colleague's phone number so I could call him for a referral. He said he didn't have the number at home, but he thought he had it at the office. I asked him if he would call and leave the number on my recorder the next day, which he agreed to do. He never did.

When I sensed I wasn't going to get any help from Tom, I called my cousin, Jim, also a psychologist, who was living in Chicago at the time. I asked him if he could help me find a therapist for Jen. He said he would make some contacts and get back with me.

He called the next day with two names. When I called Jen, she told me she'd already found a female psychologist and had an appointment to see her the following week.

In an effort to help Jennifer understand that sometimes others don't appreciate our individual gifts, I asked her, "Do you remember the story of the ugly duckling?"

"Vaguely. Tell me again."

"Remember how one little duckling always felt and looked different than the other ducks? And how being different was hard for him? One day the duckling saw his reflection in the water and realized he was a beautiful swan. That's what you are, Jen, a beautiful swan in a duck pond. Your light is just too bright for these guys. And don't forget it's tough on a man's ego for a woman to be more intelligent and talented than he is." I think she understood what I was saying—at least I hoped so.

During our subsequent conversations, I would frequently refer to her as my "Swan Princess" to help her remember who she was. I went to the bookstore and looked in the children's section to see if they carried the book, *The Ugly Duckling*. Some of the fairy tales were packaged with a stuffed animal pertinent to the story. I asked if the store could order one like that, combining *The Ugly Duckling* book with a swan stuffed animal. They said they could, and ordered it for me. I thought it would be a nice reminder for Jen to see the swan every day.

The next week I was in Dallas on business. I was a sales and management training consultant for Ford Motor Company. I called Jen at the Pentagon from a lobby pay phone during my break. There were obviously other people standing around her, and she was trying to tell me something without saying it directly.

Jen was taking a psychology course at the local university, and used a reference to the course to explain what transpired at her first meeting with the psychologist.

"My psychology professor wants me to write a paper on clinical depression."

I didn't understand initially she was talking in "code" and replied, "Oh, really?"

She knew I didn't comprehend her message, so she said, "Mom ... " in a tone of voice that told me to "Get with the program." I then understood her psychologist diagnosed her with clinical depression. She continued, "He wants the paper to include information on antidepressants."

I was standing in a hotel lobby in Dallas, with my daughter in Washington D.C., having just told me she was clinically depressed. I felt so helpless.

That evening from Dallas, I called Jen's father, Russ, and asked if Jen was still on his medical insurance. He said no. I told him Jen was depressed. I explained she was seeing a psychologist, and needed to see a psychiatrist as well for medication. I asked if he would help with the medical bills. He said yes.

As soon as I got home from Dallas, I wrote a check to Jen to cover her first psychology visit. I enclosed it in a card that said, "Angels can fly ... because they take themselves lightly." I was hoping to instill a message of not taking life too seriously. But then, I had the same problem. She and I were alike in many ways.

I was concerned about her going on medication. I was especially concerned about her carrying a weapon while taking medication.

"Are you going to tell your supervisors about the antidepressant medication?" I asked her.

"No," she replied.

"What about random drug testing?" At that point in time, drug testing was relatively new, and I knew very little about what was covered in routine testing.

"I've just been tested and I should be all right for a while," she said.

I should have been more worried about her not taking the antidepressant, but I was panicked, confused and scared.

She talked several weeks earlier about wanting to get out of the military. She was under the impression it would cost $30,000 to repay the military for her training if she left before her contract expired.

It seemed a shame this young woman, who once loved the military and serving her country, should now be so desperate and unhappy because of two or three individuals. She was certain they were out to destroy her military career, and she wasn't imagining it. There actually were derogatory conversations going on about her—undeserved, unfounded, and petty.

"Mom, they are referring to me as a 'Shit Bird.' That's the ultimate insult to a Marine!"

This bright, conscientious and talented young woman was anything but a "Shit Bird."

During the time Jen worked at the Pentagon, a new XO (Executive Officer), CWO3 (Chief Warrant Officer) Manley arrived at HMC. Jen heard that Sgt. Wesson and a Sgt. Jones had been criticizing her to the new XO. As time drew near for Jen's return to HMC, she mentioned this to Staff Sgt. Sweeney. Sweeny told her the new XO was meeting with her individual staff in an effort to get to know them better. Jen asked to speak to the new XO in person. Manley refused to see her.

The week of September 25, Jen was told she would have to report back to HMC on October second. She was seeing the psychologist frequently during this time, trying to work through all the dynamics involved with her transfer back into that caustic environment. I talked with her on Wednesday, and wasn't able to reach her over the weekend. I left several messages on her recorder. It was unusual for her not to return my calls.

On the morning of Monday, October second, the day Jen was supposed to report back to HMC, I had to be in Detroit, an hour's drive, by 8 a.m. When I awoke that morning, I felt so strongly I should send an e-mail message to everyone in my email address book, and ask them to pray for Jen. But I needed to get on the road, and I didn't think I had enough time. In addition, if I did send the prayer request, everyone would wonder why. Not following through with my intuition is another decision I will wonder about and regret, perhaps for the rest of my life.

Once I got on the road, I called Jen's room at the barracks from my car phone. No one answered. I thought she might be in the shower, so I left a message on her answering machine wishing her good luck.

On my way home from Detroit, I called her room again. It was about 5p.m. and she should have been back by then. I got her machine once again.

I proceeded with plans to take my mother to dinner. The entire time at the restaurant I thought about Jenny. I said to my mother, "I wonder if I will always have a heavy heart where Jen is concerned."

When I dropped my mother off, I said the strangest thing, "No mother should outlive her child."

I don't know why I said that. It was one of those unconscious statements one utters and then wonders where it came from. It was as if a part of me already knew.

I went to bed that evening still not hearing from Jen. I was just starting to drift off to sleep when the phone rang. I answered it but there was no one there.

A short time later, at approximately 10:30 p.m., the doorbell rang. I opened my bedroom window, which faced the front of the house, and through the screen asked who was there.

I heard Jen's father, Russ, say "It's me; open the door."

I saw two uniformed Marines, a man and a woman, standing there and I started screaming, "No, no ... "

I opened the door and jumped back continuing to shout "No, No,"— as if I could stop them from saying what I sensed was coming.

Russ walked toward me and held me, while the male Marine officer proceeded to read his statement: "This evening, at approximately 1700 hours, upon completion of sentry duty at the Naval Command Center at the Pentagon, LCpl. Jennifer Merrihew was found dead in the lavatory, from an apparent self-inflicted gunshot wound to the head."

My knees buckled and I could no longer hear the officer's voice.

−2−

Starry, Starry Night

What we can do, we do. Beyond that, we endure,
our endurance framed by a sense of what matters
and what does not.

~ Sister Wendy Beckett, *Meditations on Peace*

Russ guided me to the couch and invited the two Marine officers, one of whom was a woman, to be seated. When I collected myself enough to speak, I uttered, "The Pentagon?" I was confused. I thought she was back at HMC. No wonder I couldn't reach her that morning. She started work much earlier at the Pentagon.

When they finished their very difficult task, the casualty assistance officers asked if I had anyone who could stay with me. I asked Russ if he would stay for a while, which he agreed to. I saw the female officer glance at Jen's military picture, which was prominently displayed above the fireplace mantle. She and 1st/Sgt. Rofstetter wouldn't have known Jen personally since they were from the Toledo office. They expressed their condolences once again, and explained they would be contacting me tomorrow to talk about the preparations.

After they left, an emotional dam erupted deep inside. I didn't know which feeling to deal with first—anger, confusion, disbelief, or desperation. I kept screaming and crying, "She didn't want to go back there. Why did they make her go back there?"

Russ brought me a glass of water, but my hands were shaking too badly to hold it.

We cried, talked, and prayed for Jennifer. Finally, either Russ or I mentioned my family needed to be called. By now, it was approximately 11:30 p.m. I'm not sure who called my sister, Diane. The series of events are somewhat of a blur for me, but her call was the first we made. She came immediately.

I called my sister, Jeanne, who lives in the Detroit area. "Jeanne, is Roger with you?" Upon hearing he was I tried to continue, "Jeanne … Jeanne …. " All I could do was say her name over and over again, so Russ took the phone and told her. She and her husband, Roger drove down that night. Jeanne was Jen's godmother.

We decided to wait until morning to tell the rest of the family. There was no sense in robbing them of their sleep when there was nothing anyone could do.

Diane took Russ home and came back to stay with me. Jeanne tucked me into bed but there was no sleeping that night.

In the morning, Roger and Jeanne drove to my mother's house to tell her. I didn't know what to say to the rest of my family. Should I tell them the truth? Suicide—I couldn't even say the word.

We decided at this point to tell them we didn't have all the details yet, but she died of a bullet wound to the head. My family was making most of the calls, but there was one I wanted to try to make myself—to my stepson, Ben. He already left for school when I called, and Tom, my former husband, had left for work. I asked Tom's wife to leave a message for Ben to call me.

I called him again when I thought he would be home from school, and I was able to reach him. I composed myself and said, "Ben, I have some bad news. Jennifer is dead." I couldn't bring myself to tell him Jen shot herself. I wanted to spare him that horror. "She died from an accidental firing of a weapon."

"Are you sure?" he asked without emotion.

"Yes."

He quietly said, "I'm sorry."

His response seemed odd. I couldn't see his face and I had trouble understanding his reaction. Was he in shock like the rest of us?

"Please let me know if you need any help getting to Toledo for the funeral." I was willing to make the arrangements and to pay for his ticket if necessary. With that, we said "Goodbye."

It never occurred to me the news of her death would have reached as far as Texas, but later I found it had. We were living in the Houston area at the time Jen entered the Marine Corps, so, of course our Texas address was listed as her "home of record."

As difficult as the concept of my child killing herself was for me, and as hard as it would have been for Ben to hear, I should have told him the truth. But I hadn't even begun to digest the ramifications of it all. I was still in shock. Someone else should have made that call—someone who was thinking more clearly than I was. Perhaps the news of Jen's death had already hit Texas by the time I contacted Ben. That would account for his asking me if I was sure of her cause of death. For someone who was typically straightforward and honest, I had made a poor decision.

I was greatly concerned about the manner of Jen's death. Some religions believe the soul has a difficult transition if one commits suicide. I was raised in the Catholic faith with the belief if you commit suicide your soul goes to purgatory, never to reach heaven. Even though the church's position on suicide has softened in recent years, my "spiritual programming" did not leave me with much peace of mind.

Additionally, I was feeling intense pain with the realization my child was so unhappy, miserable, and desperate she took her own life. Where had I failed? I obsessed over every time I lost patience, every time I yelled, all the times I should have listened more and talked less. I replayed every "tough love" decision I made regarding Jennifer, and wondered if I had been wrong. I especially obsessed over that stupid letter I had written to her. I wondered if she felt like she had nowhere to go. Maybe if I hadn't written the letter, she would have felt like she had a home to come to. I wasn't thinking clearly. I wasn't remembering the multitude of positive letters, conversations, and words of love we exchanged before and after *the* letter.

I regretted marrying Tom. Maybe we wouldn't have moved to Texas if I hadn't. Perhaps she wouldn't have joined the Marine Corps if I had stayed with her in Toledo. All of the *if onlys* and more were going through my head.

Within the first few hours of the devastating news, not only did I pray for God to take her into the light, I begged Him for a sign she was with Him. I didn't have too wait long for the sign. Two days after Jen passed, my sister Bobbi came over. She shared a conversation she had with her daughter Lindsay, who was five at the time.

"Mamma," Lindsay said. "I dreamed about Jennifer. She was up in heaven with Grandpa Robert [my father] and Sarge [the family dog who passed]. They were watching over the whole earth!"

Jennifer with Sarge

More tears sprang to my already red and swollen eyes. That was my sign! Bobbi had not known of my request to God—nobody did.

I believe God and our loved ones communicate to us through dreams. Often children are more receptive to those types of messages because they don't have all the blocks and barriers adults do.

I had mentioned to my family to be open to the possibility Jen might communicate to them through dreams, and to share them with me if they occurred. And now, this angel child was passing on a message from my angel child. To not only mention Jen was in heaven, but also with my father, gave it even more credence. Little did I know her comment about Sarge would later be profoundly validated.

I thought of how sensitive Jen always was, right from the time she was little. If there was a wounded bird lying in the yard, she insisted we drive twenty miles to an animal shelter where it could be cared for. She loved animals and had talked about becoming a veterinarian. She later changed her mind when she began to have allergies to certain animals. She decided to become an English teacher, but her love for animals continued.

In those early days following Jen's death, as I sat with my family trying to come to terms with what had happened, the words from the song, "Vincent" about Vincent van Gogh, kept going through my head. I told my sister Diane, "The song seems to speak for Jennifer, too. 'When all hope was lost in sight, on that starry, starry night, you took your life as lovers often do. But I could have told you [Jennifer], this world was never meant for one as beautiful as you.'"[1]

The primal, guttural sobs coming from deep within me, I never heard come out of a human. I sounded like a wounded animal. I begged and pleaded with God to give me another chance. I wanted her back. I was inconsolable. The pain was beyond description. I thought, *If I have to live with this pain the rest of my life, then I deserve an easy death.* In the next minute I was yelling at God, "You owe me a heart attack in my sleep."

On Wednesday Russ and I met with 1st/Sgt. Rofstetter, the Casualty Assistance Officer, to make plans for the funeral. He told us that, due to the nature of her wounds, Jen would have a closed casket. Her father and I began to sob. We would never again see her, never hold her.

Seeing our strong reaction, Sgt. Rofstetter said, "I'll check with the coroner once again to see if there is any way you can see her."

As much as I wanted to see her, I also wanted to remember her lovely face as I last saw it, not one that was wounded and swollen. Those were not images I wanted to stay with me the rest of my life.

Sgt. Rofstetter continued. "The earliest her body could be flown home is Friday."

We were not prepared to have to wait so long. We composed ourselves, and decided, given that information, to have the viewing on Friday evening with the funeral on Saturday.

I mentioned to Russ, "Maybe waiting until Saturday for the funeral service might be better after all. Perhaps more friends and family would be able to attend a Saturday funeral than one during the week. Besides, the delay would give me more time to compose myself."

Sgt. Rofstetter continued, "Jennifer is entitled to a full military funeral. Would you like that?

We both agreed without hesitation. Jen deserved that.

"I will provide the military pallbearers. Do you want a 21-gun salute?"

We paused, and said, "Yes."

Sgt. Rofstetter nodded silently and made a note. He reviewed his list and asked "Is there anything else I can do for you?"

"I never got a video copy of Jen's graduation ceremony from Parris Island," I said. "Is it still possible to get a copy?" I gave him the date of her graduation, as well as her platoon number.

"I will certainly try."

I continued, "Jen has a good friend in the Marines who needs to be notified of her death. His name is Cpl. Tristin Powers. I have no idea where he is stationed. Could you locate him and let him know about Jen? Please ask him to call me."

Sgt. Rofstetter nodded as he wrote down the information. He then wrapped up the conversation.

When we met the next day, Sgt. Rofstetter handed me a videotape of Jen's graduation and said, "I felt the chances were very slim I would be able to obtain this because copies of each graduation aren't routinely kept on file. A drill instructor did not want her copy, so there just happened to be one left on the shelf."

I felt the hand of God at that moment. He knew someday I would want this tape. My thoughts drifted to Jen's graduation from boot camp that day in July 1994. She had been selected as the Honor Graduate for her Platoon. The recipient of this award is one who "demonstrates a high degree of discipline, proficiency, bearing, and physical fitness."

Jennifer kept the award a secret until the day before graduation, as she was showing her father and me around the base. Russ, who also served in the Marine Corps, was not in earshot when she told me. She wanted him to be surprised.

Russ Merrihew and LCpl Jennifer Merrihew in front of the
Iwo Jima Statue at Parris Island following her graduation

I was very proud of her, and she was so elated and excited as she shared the news. I came to her graduation straight from a business trip in New Orleans and had been on the road for ten days. Unknown to me, waiting at home was a letter from her superiors, informing me she had been chosen as Honor Graduate, and Russ and I were invited to sit in the VIP pavilion during the ceremony.

I did not know videotapes of the ceremony would be available until afterward when I saw a sign to that effect while shopping at the base exchange. I asked Jen if she ordered one, and she said, "No." I was disappointed to hear that, especially in lieu of her awards.

Each Honor Graduate was awarded a complimentary set of dress blues. During the graduation ceremony, Jen wore her dress blues and marched separately from her platoon. She was honored with two awards in front of the entire assembly. One was in recognition of her Honor Graduate status. The other, the Marksmanship Award, was presented for achieving the highest score of her platoon on the rifle range.

My thoughts shifted from one of the proudest moments of my life, to the stark reality she had turned her gun against herself and would be buried in her dress blues.

−3−

A Closed Casket

God, grant me the serenity
to accept the things I cannot change,
the courage to change the things I can,
and the wisdom to know the difference.

~ Serenity Prayer

"**I** was able to locate Cpl. Powers at Camp Pendleton in San Diego," Sgt. Rofstetter continued. "He has been informed and he will be calling you. However, the Marine Corps cannot pay for his flight, since he is not immediate family."

"I understand," I replied. I'm just grateful you were able to locate him."

Tristin called later that day. "Hi Mom," he said softly.

He always called me Mom, which tickled me. I would have loved to have him as a son-in-law.

"My CO told me the bad news. I'm so sorry. I want to come for the funeral. My superiors have granted me leave."

"I'll pay for the airfare."

"We could use the travel service that is available to the military."

I gave him my credit card number so he could make the arrangements. He couldn't talk long and said he would call when he knew his flight plans.

I hung up and remembered utilizing that same travel service around the time Tristin was graduating from boot camp. I had given Jen one of my frequent flyer tickets so she could attend his graduation at Camp Pendleton. Jen was so excited about going. I called the travel agency to check on hotel room availability but they were sold out. I later talked with Tristin's mother who said Jen could share a room with Melissa, Tristin's sister.

Jen came home from Tristin's graduation very excited and impressed with the ceremony. It was Jen who influenced Tristin to enter the Marines, and following his graduation she finalized her decision to join the Corps, although she didn't tell me until March of 1994—after she enlisted.

I remember every detail of the conversation. I walked into my bedroom in Houston when the phone rang. Jen's voice was a mixture of excitement and hesitation. "Mom, are you sitting down?"

"It sounds like I should be," I replied as I sat on the edge of the bed.

"I enlisted in the Marine Corps."

I sucked in my breath, fortunately not audibly, and weighed my next words carefully. I realized it was a *fait accompli* and there was nothing I could do to change the situation. The best I could do was to support her decision.

"Tell me why you joined."

"I know I need to learn respect for authority," she said, as I grinned and nodded. "And I need to learn discipline."

Jen was always insightful, but that degree of self-introspection I felt was rare in someone barely eighteen. Her reasons were solid … *but the Marines! Nothing like picking the toughest branch of the military, and one with the fewest number of women!*

"I'm proud of you," I said. "You have assessed your areas for growth and are tackling them head-on. When do you go in?"

"I go to boot camp in April."

That was only a month away. Tom and I had been sleeping in separate rooms and, by then, I had made plans to move back to the Toledo area.

My focus returned to the present where I was now in Michigan planning my daughter's funeral, and trying to make arrangements for Tristin. But the past was surely more comforting, and I let my thoughts wander to the first time we met Tristin. It was January 1993. Tom had accepted the position in Texas, and we just moved into our new house. We were still in the process of unpacking boxes.

Jennifer did not want to move from Toledo to Texas. She was in the middle of her junior year in high school. She wanted to finish school in Toledo and did not want to leave her friends. My greatest concern was how the move would affect her. When I told her about the move she burst into tears. We were standing outside of our home in Toledo. We walked around the house several times as we talked. It was more like pacing than walking. I told her I wouldn't force her to go and we would talk with her father about her staying in Toledo long enough to finish high school. In the end, Jen made the decision to go to Texas.

Tom and Ben were adjusting well, but Jen and I struggled. We were leaving family and friends. Tom's family was not from the Toledo area, so the move didn't have the same impact on him. In fact, he was looking forward to getting out of Toledo. Ben just started his freshman year, so he hadn't been as integrated into the school as Jen was. I wanted her to make new friendships as soon as possible.

I was standing in the front yard shortly after we moved, when I saw a handsome young man with blond hair walking toward me. He looked about the same age as Jen, and I later learned he was a year older. I introduced myself and told him we just moved in.

He told me his name was Tristin. "I live at the end of the street," he said as he pointed to his house.

"I have two children I would like you to meet." I called to Jen and Ben asking them to come outside. They gave me that, *Oh, Mom* look, but they came. It wasn't long before the three of them were fast friends.

Later that day, Jen got cleaned up and went down to the subdivision's mailboxes across from Tristin's house. She was hoping Tristin would come outside. She said she wanted a chance to redeem herself, since when Tristin first saw her, she was "grubby."

Tristin and Jen began dating and fell in love. That spring they went to the prom together. Jen wore a short royal blue velvet dress with spaghetti straps. It was scalloped at the bottom with beaded fringe of the same color. We went to several stores before we found shoes to match.

Tristin wore a white tux, with a vest and bow tie that matched the color of Jen's dress. They were a striking couple—she with her dark hair and brown eyes, and he with his blond hair and blue eyes. I took several pictures in front of our house. Tristin's parents were there with their camera as well. Tristin was a senior and would be graduating in June. Jen was talking to him about military service.

Military service ... I was back to the present. There was much to do to get ready for Jen's funeral. Sgt. Rofstetter told us her body would be flown from Washington to the Toledo Airport. I told him I wanted to be there to meet her casket. Later, he told us Jen would be flown into Detroit, fifty miles away. That complicated matters and we weren't able to coordinate my presence.

We decided to have Jen's funeral at St. Ignatius, my family's church, and to bury her next to my father in the church cemetery. My family and I purchased a second adjoining plot when we bought Dad's. How could I have known we would be burying my child there? Who could have predicted the whole natural order would become completely out of synch?

Russ, Jeanne, and I went to the mortuary to choose Jen's casket and to make the arrangements. On the holy card with her name, which was to be given to those attending the visitation, I chose to have the *Serenity Prayer*: "God grant me the serenity to accept the things I cannot change, the courage to change the things I can, and the wisdom to know the difference." I felt that prayer summarized it all. How was I ever going to accept this? Where would I find the courage and strength to go on?

From the mortuary, Jeanne and I went to the church to see the priest and discuss the funeral arrangements. After some preliminary information was obtained, Fr. Al said, "Would you like to choose the Gospel readings?

"Father," I replied, "I can't make any more decisions at this point. Would you please choose them for me?"

He nodded.

"There are, however, two songs I would like played at some point during the funeral, 'You'll Never Walk Alone' from *Carousel,* and 'I'll Walk with God' from *The Student Prince.*" I needed to be reminded I wouldn't truly be alone.

"I'll see what I can do," Father replied.

"Would you give the eulogy?" I continued.

"Sure. Please make a few notes for me."

We went back to my brother Patrick's house, which was our childhood home. It was just down the street from the church. Several of my family members were there. I asked them to share with me memories of Jen, which they began to do. As they did, I took notes and later wrote the eulogy from the notes. I also wrote her obituary. Why I felt I needed to do all this, I don't know. I guess it helped me feel as if I was doing something for her. I would never again be able to comb her hair, never cook another meal for her, never wash her clothes ... but I could write her eulogy. Besides, I felt no one knew her better than I did.

We needed to decide about memorial donations. I was currently serving on the "Wish Granting" committee for the *Make-A-Wish Foundation,* which grants wishes to children who have life threatening or terminal illnesses. Her father and I decided memorial contributions made in Jennifer's name would be directed there. Much later, I thought about the paradox of all that—I also had a child who for a short time was terminally ill. I just didn't know it at the time.

Jeanne and I stopped at the florist. Jen loved roses. I ordered two-dozen red roses from her father and me, with a ribbon saying, "Daughter."

As we left the floral shop I said, "Jeanne, I have to find a swan to nestle among the roses." We searched through gift shops until we found a mother and baby swan together, sitting on a wooden stand under a glass dome. It was perfect. I took the smaller swan back to the florist and asked her to tie it in among the roses for my "Swan Princess."

That evening, my friend Linda stopped by. She and I had performed together in a number of musical shows with a nearby community theater group. She shared with me that when she told her daughter Laura, about Jen's passing, Laura replied, "I always thought Jen was so neat. She used to make Dorito sandwiches when we were at the theater together."

"I never knew that," I said. "There must be dozens of 'Jenny stories' I know nothing about."

I wanted to hear them all. I wanted to know everything anyone had to say about her. I was desperate to capture and preserve every memory. I decided to have papers available at the mortuary on which visitors could write their favorite memory of Jennifer. Jeanne, who was staying with me, volunteered to create a form.

"Jeanne, since the casket will be closed, let's display pictures of Jen all over the room." My family and I told everyone we talked with to bring to the mortuary his or her favorite picture of Jen in a frame. Jeanne went to a local store and bought as many frames as she could find. They came in different sizes, shapes, colors and patterns. I thought they were beautiful.

I previously made a collage of Jen's school pictures, which was hanging in my home. Her senior picture was in the middle, and her photos from kindergarten through high school were placed in a circle around

Joyce and Jennifer

her senior picture. I decided to take that one with me, as well as a five-by-seven picture of Jen with her horse at summer camp. Jen loved animals, especially horses.

There was someone from my family with me at all times. Five of my six brothers and sisters, as well as my mother, lived within a seventy-mile radius, so they took turns staying with me. They prepared the meals and answered the phone. Occasionally I would take a call.

Many of my friends stopped by the house. With every new arrival, the deep, guttural sobbing would begin all over again. Each time I talked about Jen, it was as if a geyser in me would erupt. It must have been excruciating for my family to see me like this. After several hours, my sister Diane couldn't bear to see me go through this anymore, so she began telling people they shouldn't come to the house.

I overheard her say that to someone on the phone. When she hung up, I said to her, "Diane, I know this is hard on you. Maybe you need to take a break. Why don't you go home for a while and rest?"

She said she wanted to stay.

When my friend Colleen came over, we went back in Jen's bedroom and shut the door, so my sister wouldn't have to listen to my wailing. Diane knocked softly, came in and said to me, "This is *your* house. If you need to cry, you don't have to come back here to do it."

Diane left us to our privacy. I can only now begin to imagine how helpless my family must have felt.

I said to Colleen, "Jen's suicide has reached the national news," and hung my head. I was devastated. I am a very private person and this seemed so heartless.

Colleen said the wisest thing to me, "Well, now that everyone knows, they can all be supportive."

I didn't realize until later how right she was. How long would I have tried to keep Jen's suicide a secret? How long would I have tried to carry that baggage? The decision was made for me.

Colleen continued, "Joyce, no one is judging you. No one thinks this is your fault. We all love you and we know you were a good mother. No one is judging Jennifer either. She was sick. She was depressed. Her depression killed her, just like a cancer would."

But what caused her depression? Was it nature or nurture? Was it the harassment and irresponsibility of a few members of the military? Was it her inability to protect herself from a person like Dick, and if so, where did that come from? How did she get mixed up with a guy like him in the first place? These were questions I would continue to wrestle with for a long time to come. But for now, I needed to take some of the most difficult steps of my life. I had to face my daughter's casket.

−4−
Saying Good-Bye

Grief is about unfinished business.
All that still aches to be done, said, or felt together.
The possibilities that will never be realized must
now be surrendered, but our unfinished
connection will quietly accompany the
remainder of my own journey.

~ Molly Fumia, *Safe Passage*

Friday afternoon, I walked into the mortuary with my family. We were to have private visiting time before the doors would be open to the public. My sister Bobbi and my brother-in-law Mark were holding on to me. I saw two Marine Honor Guards standing at the doorway. I started to walk forward but my knees buckled. I grabbed hold of my sister and brother-in-law's arms. They walked me through the door and up to her flag-draped coffin. I knelt down in front of it and put my head on the coffin. I wanted to touch her, to hold her, to stroke her hair. I wanted to see those beautiful brown eyes again. I wanted to turn back the clock. I wanted my daughter back.

Russ approached and said, "I asked to see Jennifer. Joyce, she looks fine. Her mouth is a little swollen, but she really looks like herself."

"Oh … that's good. You were brave to do that. Thank you for telling me." It never occurred to me I could ask to see her as well. I was still in shock.

Months later, when I continued to agonize over not having seen her, I asked Russ, "Did it help you to see her?"

"Not really," he responded.

The room was filled with flowers and pictures of Jen. A second adjoining room had to be opened just to accommodate the flowers and the people who came. I walked around the rooms, looking at all the flowers and reading the cards that came with them. It brought much comfort to see how many people had sent flowers. It was like getting a hug from each one of them, and it was certainly a wonderful tribute to Jen, as was the number of people who came to pay their respects. Her friends from high school, teachers, and previous neighbors continued to file into the room. Several of her friends from the military were there in uniform. Most of them were Marines, but there was one young man in a white naval uniform.

Sgt. Rofstetter picked up Tristin from the airport in Toledo and took him to his hotel. I was grateful for that. Tristin had gotten a ride to the mortuary with some of Jen's other military friends who were staying at the same hotel. He walked into the room wearing his dress blues, and we embraced. He stood by my side for the next two days.

People poured in and stayed. It seemed as if no one could leave. They walked around and looked at Jen's pictures. They wrote their memories of Jen and put them in the basket provided. They talked with Jen's friends. I had hoped Ben and Tom would come, but they didn't.

I was meeting Jen's military friends for the first time. A young Marine, Michelle, who bore a striking resemblance to Jen, approached me. "I'm Michelle, a friend of Jen's. I am Jen's Military Escort and I accompanied her body from Washington." Jen mentioned Michelle several times and I knew they had been close friends. Michelle presented me with Jen's

Honor Graduate and National Defense medals. I carried them with me the rest of the evening.

A young Marine with flaming red hair was crying uncontrollably. I approached her. "I'm Amy," she said. I was Jen's roommate." I held her as she continued to sob.

In the morning we had a brief visitation at the mortuary, then went to St. Ignatius Church for the funeral service. Jen's casket was wheeled to the front of the church where Russ and I placed a white cloth over it, as was tradition for a Catholic funeral. As I turned to walk to my seat in the first row, I noticed the church was full. Father Al began to read the eulogy:

> *Jennifer was a diverse and unique individual. She was extremely sensitive, with a tough exterior. This is a person, who after a 20-hour Nintendo marathon with her Aunt Diane would get up early in the morning to go fishing with her father.*
>
> *She often went to theater rehearsals with her mother. At a rehearsal for* Annie Get Your Gun, *when Jen was only four-years-old, she recited all of Joyce's lines verbatim, much to the amazement of the cast.*
>
> *She loved singing and had a beautiful voice. She sang the National Anthem a cappella at the start of her high school volleyball games in Texas. She also sang at two of her aunt's weddings. She was very active in Sylvania Northview's Harmony Road Show singing group. After the move to Texas, Jen's mother surprised her for her seventeenth birthday and sent her to Chicago to meet her Harmony Road Show friends who were there on tour.*
>
> *Her commitment and love for family was demonstrated when she drove seventeen hours non-stop from Texas to be with her family for Easter breakfast. She took advantage of every moment she had to be with family.*
>
> *She was a very loving person. Bobbi recalls that when she was pregnant with Brandon, Jen always brought a gift for him.*

Jennifer loved horses and spent summers volunteering at the horse stables at Camp Storer. Much to her mother's amazement, she won an award for the cleanest horse stall. Joyce often wondered if she put a sign saying "Barn" over Jen's bedroom, if that would help Jen keep it clean.

In April of 1994 Jennifer entered the Marine Corps. She was one of the 50% of her platoon who graduated from boot camp. She was selected as the Honor Graduate, and was one of only two women who wore "dress blues" at the ceremony, where she was presented two awards. She was proud to serve her country, and we are all proud of her. She was loved by many and will certainly be missed."

Throughout the eulogy, people cried, laughed, then cried again. Upon conclusion of the mass, the white cloth covering the casket was replaced with the United States flag. As the military honor guard wheeled her casket down the aisle, Russ and I followed closely behind. We had been married in this church, but this walk down the aisle held none of the happiness of that day, which seemed so long ago. As the procession made its way to the old country cemetery behind the church, I held Tristin's arm.

We gathered around the casket under the tent. The mournful notes of *Taps* were played. The same song that signaled bedtime on the base was now serenading Jen as she was laid to her final rest, only this time it was played in a different key ... one that mirrored the somber mood of those present. The twenty-one-gun salute followed. Too many people, including her father and me, winced every time the rifles fired. It was a striking reminder of the way she died. It was meant as a salute to her, but it was extremely unsettling.

The flag from her coffin was folded and Sgt. Rofstetter presented it to me saying, "This flag is being presented to you by a grateful nation, for the honorable and faithful service performed by Lance Corporal Jennifer Merrihew." A second flag was folded and presented to her father. The graveside services had ended.

It was time for me to leave but my feet were like stone. I couldn't move. How could I leave her here? How could I walk away from my child—just like that? I looked behind me to see a multitude of people waiting to pay their last respects. If I didn't move, they couldn't get to the casket. I turned to Diane and said, "I suppose I have to leave now." She nodded. I lifted one foot and then the other. I turned and walked away. As I came out from under the tent, it began to rain. How appropriate the skies should cry as well.

The wake was held at my brother Patrick's house, just down the street from the church. It was the house where my six siblings and I were raised. Patrick and Stacy (my future sister-in-law) did a wonderful job of serving the food and hosting the guests. And they "entertained" Jen's friends from the Marine Corps.

I sat on the couch in the living room by myself. Tristin checked on me now and then.

Later that evening, Tristin and I walked back to the grave. We spent some quiet time there by ourselves. As we prepared to leave, we each took a rose from the bouquet I purchased from the florist, which had been transported to the gravesite. By now, I just wanted to go home. I wanted to be by myself. I wanted this day to be over. I wanted my life to be over. I wanted to hold her. I wanted anything but this.

Tristin said he would ride home with me and stay until Jeanne and Roger, who were staying overnight, returned. When we arrived at my home, there was an awkward pause, as if to say, "What do we do now?"

Tristin told me Jen used to hang roses upside down to dry them. I hung mine over the kitchen sink.

Tristin and I talked until Jeanne and her husband Roger come home from Patrick's house. As they were getting ready to take Tristin back to the hotel, I thanked him for his support, saying I would see him in the morning. I took a sleeping pill and went to bed, hoping and praying I would not awaken—or if I did, I would find all of this to be a horrible nightmare.

−5−

The Punch
in the Gut

To suffer passes. But to have suffered, never passes.

~ Unknown

Within seconds of waking the next morning, the realization of Jen's death crashed over me like a giant tidal wave, a steamroller, a runaway train. I felt as if I were being punched in the gut. This sensation occurred every time I awakened, whether it was in the middle of the night, which happened often, or early in the morning. I came to call this the "Double *Oh God* feeling": "Oh, God, this wasn't a dream. She's really dead! Oh, God ... I wish I hadn't awakened."

Several of Jen's military friends stayed at the hotel the night of the funeral. Some of them flew from Washington D.C., while others had driven. On Sunday they came over to my house. Meredith, a beautiful young woman with long, dark curly hair, had been taking classes with Jen at the local university in Virginia. She was engaged and her fiancé was with her. Jen was to have been one of her bridesmaids. Michelle and Tristin also came, as well as a young woman named Teresa.

They wanted to look at pictures of Jen. They sat on the floor and pored through photo albums. They asked me questions about her childhood. I filled in some of those pieces for them, and they shared with me stories of her military life. They asked if they could read the memories people had written at the mortuary. I got them out and we took turns reading them out loud. I couldn't do much reading.

One of Tristin's memories was playing Trivial Pursuit at our house while eating Mint Milano cookies and drinking coffee. He also wrote about prom night and the first day he met all of us. He mentioned Jen's beautiful singing voice, and how competitive she was.

Meredith wrote about Jen going to "every bridal store in Northern Virginia with me so she could help pick out her bridesmaid dress for my wedding."

There were stories of volleyball games, swim meets, school plays, sleepovers, pranks on the pizza delivery boy, and of the cross-stitched gifts Jen made. What emerged as the memories were read was a profile of a young woman with a wonderful sense of humor, who was always help-ing someone out of a rut, and who loved to sing and dance, especially to country and western music. It was the portrait of a person who was full of life. What had happened? How could all that life be gone?

I had many questions, especially regarding the military. Why hadn't someone stopped the harassment by Sgt. Wesson? Why was Jen forced back into that environment?

Michelle shared with me a conversation she had with Dick right after they were informed of Jennifer's death. Dick told her Jen called him at HMC just before she died. Jen asked him if they were going to treat her fairly if she came back to work there. She was referring to Sgt. Wesson, Sgt. Jones and the new XO, CWO Manley. Dick apparently told her, "If you act like a Marine, they will treat you like a Marine."

"Jen said to him, 'I hope you remember the last time you saw me, because no one will ever see me again,'" Michelle continued.

"Dick was concerned with her statement because of her previous suicide attempt. He reported the phone call to Sgt. Wesson and then to CWO Manley. Manley did nothing with the information. She and everyone else involved with that call knew about Jennifer's previous suicide attempt. They had time to make a call and have Jen's weapon confiscated. But they did nothing." Michelle began to sob as I held her, my heart so heavy.

Where was the leadership in this organization? Was there no one who was thinking clearly? Were they all so absorbed in their own "stuff" they couldn't hear the desperate cries of this young woman, who was once at the top of her class? How do people with such poor management skills get in leadership positions? Didn't they know this young Marine was a human being with feelings and fears, or doesn't the military care? Didn't they know she had a family who loved her and would have done anything to help her? Why didn't she call one of us who cared about her? Why did she make her last call to an office that didn't give a damn about her?

Many of her military friends were disappointed and disillusioned with the Corps. Their lives had been turned upside-down by her death and the way her situation was handled, or more notably, *not* handled. They, as well as her school friends, needed a place to grieve, someone to talk with about their feelings. My home became a venue for that.

The following day, on Monday I took Michelle and Theresa back to the Detroit airport. They promised to keep in touch. I hated to see her friends go. I wanted them to stay longer. Seeing them leave was like letting another part of Jen go.

The next day I took Tristin to the Toledo airport for his return to Camp Pendleton. Friends and family volunteered to take him, but I declined their offer. I wanted to spend as much time with him as I could.

We approached the ticket counter to check his bags. There were military rules he had to follow with respect to checking his dress blues and his cover (hat). We were trying to figure out the best way to do this. The ticket agent became impatient and curt with us, even though there was no one else waiting in line.

I thought, *Sir, if you only knew what we have just gone through, you'd be much more compassionate and helpful.* Tristin decided to put his uniform in one of the garment boxes provided by the airline and to carry his cover with him.

We sat in the gate area holding hands tightly. Both of us knew in our hearts we may never see each other again, but neither one of us dared to verbalize it. When it was time for him to board, I could barely let him go. It seemed as if I were putting the last remnants of my previous life onto that plane. I hugged him good-bye and watched him walk down the Jetway holding onto his cover. I couldn't control my tears.

A young couple, who had apparently been watching the scene, walked up to me. Judging by the short hair cut on the young man, I guessed he might also be in the military. They were in the process of boarding the same flight. They looked at me with compassion and said, "Don't worry, Mom. We'll take care of him."

I thanked them and walked quickly to my car as deep, guttural sobs began to pour forth once again. Even in the midst of my sobbing, I thought of the enormous difference between their sensitivity and kindness, and the ticket agent's curt manner. They obviously assumed this was my son. Their kindness was greatly appreciated nonetheless.

I drove home to an empty house, not having a clue how I would ever be able to go on with my life. I wasn't sure I wanted to. I now understood how Jen could have felt so much pain she wanted to end her life. If only I could figure out a way to die naturally, without committing suicide. I certainly did not want to put my family and friends through more pain and grief.

Every bone, every muscle, every cell in my body ached—the kind of aching one feels with the flu. It's as if my entire body was crying out for her. I was feeling grief at a cellular level. If I ever had any doubts about the link between the mind, body, and soul, I certainly didn't now.

I was exhausted. I lay in bed and said the rosary for Jen. I asked everyone on the other side—my father, Grandma Alice, Jesus, and Mother Mary—to give Jen a hug for me, a "spiritual group hug." I would have much preferred to be hugging her myself. In time, mercifully, sleep came—for a few hours anyway.

– 6 –

Kitty

Grief, like regret,
settles into our DNA
and remains forever a part of us.

~ Kristin Hannah, *The Nightingale*

I awakened early the next morning, only to be greeted with the familiar bash in the stomach, as once again the reality of Jen's death hit me. I made my way to the kitchen and brewed a cup of coffee. I opened the French doors to the three-season porch, which provided a panorama of my backyard. The orange and yellow of the autumn leaves painted a stark contrast to the gray of my world.

As I sipped my coffee, I thought of Russ's thoughtfulness. He was notified first by the casualty assistance officers. Though we had been divorced for close to eighteen years, he was at my side to help me absorb the shock of the news, where I would have otherwise been alone.

Russ and I married in 1972, shortly after I graduated from St. Vincent Hospital School of Nursing in Toledo. I was 21 and he was 23. As soon as I passed my state boards, I would be a registered nurse (RN).

I worked for two years at St. Vincent Hospital on a step-down coronary unit. I was then recruited to teach coronary care nursing for a program that was sponsored through the American Heart Association. At that time, hospitals were just beginning to add coronary care units, and the need for training of nurses was great. I taught RNs from hospitals throughout northwest Ohio who would be working in critical care areas. I loved teaching. I taught nurses how to read rhythm strips, cardiac monitors, how to interpret heart and lung sounds, and what to do when a patient has a cardiac arrest.

A few years later, as the last few months of the American Heart Association program drew to a close, I was asked to interview for the position of Supervisor of CCU and step-down CCU at The Toledo Hospital. I was awarded the position. Middle management is always a tough position, especially in a critical care unit. I was responsible for 28 beds and 78 employees.

In December of 1986 I married Tom, who was a chaplain at Toledo Hospital. He had a Masters of Divinity and was working on his PhD in psychology. We had known each other for several years. I would frequently call on him when there was a death in the CCU. We became friends over the years.

Healthcare marketing was an area I aspired to, so when an opportunity presented in the marketing department at Toledo Hospital, I interviewed for the position and was chosen. I worked there several years, enjoying one promotion during that time.

While working full time, I was also performing in community theatre, one of my passions. I often landed leading roles in musicals, such as "Annie Get Your Gun." Jenny would often go to rehearsals with me and knew my lines as well as I did. Jenny was only four years old the first time I played the role of Annie. One evening during rehearsals for "Annie" my leading man Keith and I were rehearsing lines in the hallway of the theatre and Jen was nearby. I said my line and was waiting for him to say his when Jenny said, "Now honey, you know you shouldn't be toting no gun."

Keith wasn't paying any attention to her and was still groping for his line. Jenny repeated, "Now honey, you know you shouldn't be toting no gun."

At that point I started laughing and said, "Keith, Jenny just gave you your line."

Years later Jen would have Keith as a music teacher at her high school. He recognized her last name and he told her she used to give him his lines!

In 1989 I made, what I considered to be, a courageous move. I had been considering working for myself. I was a hard worker and I got tired of making other people rich! I thought of the various training films one watches in the medical world. I often found the films where the spokesperson was a medical person to be boring because the presenter was stiff. I decided there had to be a market for a nurse-actress.

I called a friend, Tom who was the CEO of an advertising company and asked how one got started in the acting business. He suggested I sign up with a talent agent and gave me a name of an agent in Toledo. I called her and asked for an appointment. She asked me, "Do you have a portfolio?"

Oh no! I thought. I responded, "Of course." We set the date for the meeting.

Getting off the phone I shouted to no one in particular, "What's a portfolio?"

I called Tom back and asked him. He explained it was a collection of pictures of your work, including your headshot in a nice presentation case.

I called a friend who was a photographer who agreed to take the headshot. I knew nothing about proper makeup or hair styles. However, I chose one of the pictures, placed it in the leather case I purchased with plastic sleeves, along with some pictures from plays in which I performed, and other marketing pieces for which I happened to be the subject.

When I met with the agent, she looked at my portfolio, looked at me and said, "You are much prettier than your picture. Get your headshot redone and come back and see me."

It took four headshots and some lessons in make-up application to get the "right look." I signed up with six talent agents and took a day off now and then to audition. I landed a few roles in medical training films, but to my surprise, also in television and radio commercials. Eventually, I had enough confidence to tender my resignation at Toledo Hospital and go out on my own. I left behind my reliable paycheck, company car with phone, medical insurance, and sec-

Joyce Harvey

retary. Ouch! Of course, Tom's salary helped provide somewhat of a cushion.

My first television commercial was Screen Actors Guild (SAG) job. I was not yet a member of SAG, so I was required to sign a must-join affidavit, which stated that with the next SAG job I did I would have to join the union.

At the time, SAG dues were approximately $800.00 to join and yearly dues were based on one's earnings. I began to put the money I earned from acting jobs in a savings account so I could join SAG when the time came. When I was cast in the next SAG commercial, which was relatively quickly, I was ready with the money. I also joined the American Federation of Television and Radio Artists (AFTRA) soon after, which covered every other media except film.

None of the money I spent on headshots, photographers, or dues came from the family funds. I waited until I had enough money saved from acting jobs before I paid that second, or third or fourth photographer, or ordered more headshots.

Working with three talent agents in Detroit, I began auditioning more frequently for projects related to the automotive industry. In 1990 I worked on a product launch for the 1991 Explorer, where I would present features of the vehicle to focus groups who would then be able to drive the Explorer following the presentation. I worked with a team that covered several cities, so I was quite familiar with the Explorer.

I was then chosen as a "model" or narrator for the auto circuit for Ford Motor Company, with the Explorer as my focus vehicle. I gave my presentation on the turnstile every thirty minutes pointing out the features on the Explorer. Ford's marketing approach that year shifted from having the traditional model on the turnstile to matching a spokesperson with the vehicle. I believe they called it a "Slice of Life." They matched a rugged looking guy with the F-150 or Ranger.

For the Explorer, they wanted the cross between a "soccer mom" and a professional woman. The man conducting the auditions asked me how old I was. I replied, "You can't ask me that."

He explained, "I need you to be young enough to have children playing soccer."

"If I look the part, then cast me. If I don't, then don't!" I was cast for the four major cities: New York, Chicago, Detroit, and Cleveland. One of the Cleveland newspapers did a piece titled, "Ford Dumps Models; Hires Actors." Following one of my presentations in Cleveland, a gentleman approached the turnstile, asked me several questions about the Explorer, which I answered. His final question was, "Can you shift into four-low on-the-fly?"

I answered, "No. You have to stop; shift into neutral, and then shift into four-low."

He nodded his head, confirming I was right and replied excitedly, as if he caught me in some trick, "I thought you were an actor!"

"I am," I smiled.

Every year auto manufacturers hold a new vehicle introduction show for the dealers. In 1991 I was chosen to present the features of the revised 1992 Ford Taurus at the Ford Introduction Show in Las Vegas. Following one of my presentations, a gentleman asked to speak to me.

He introduced himself, explaining he (John) worked with Ford in the Education and Training Department in Detroit.

"I am impressed with your presentation skills," John said. "Would you be interested in doing training for Ford on an ongoing basis?"

"Why don't we set a meeting in Detroit where we can discuss it further," I suggested.

We exchanged business cards.

I met with John and began to work as an independent contractor for Ford Education and Training. I was the first female contract trainer hired, so I had to prove myself—not only with my peers, but also with the sales consultants and managers in my classrooms. Much to my surprise, I learned it didn't take long for me to become one of the most requested trainers in the country.

A blur across my outside deck interrupted my reverie and brought me back to the present. I saw the kitten again. She first appeared the day after Jen died. One of my family members spotted the kitten outside on the back deck and had asked me who she belonged to. I didn't know. I had never seen her before.

Over the next few weeks, the kitten, which we soon began referring to as Kitty, would come and go. I would sit outside on the front step during the warm October days, and Kitty would be there with me, although she would not let me pet her. She would cautiously move as close to me as she could, staying just out of reach. We played a little game, where I pretended that I wasn't paying attention to her, and she would subsequently inch closer.

One evening, a friend came over to be with me. He suggested we pick up a video to watch. As we walked out to the car, Kitty meowed as if she were irritated that I was leaving. My friend suggested she might be hungry. I, who had a hard time remembering I needed to eat, certainly did not think about feeding this kitten. We picked up some cat food at the store and gave it to her upon our return. She gratefully ate it all.

The kitten continued to come and go, but she seemed to appear most often at what I began to call my "intense Jenny moments." The first time

I noticed it, I was standing in the doorway of Jen's room, looking at her things and sobbing. I looked up at the window and saw Kitty sitting on the ledge staring right at me.

I had a similar experience the evening my friend, Gail, suggested it might be good for me to get out and see a movie. Gail and I had been friends since I was twenty-one. She was a critical care nurse and had been my instructor when I attended coronary care classes through the American Heart Association. When she moved on to another project, I took her place teaching the same classes. We had been through a lot together.

I had to be very careful about what I watched, since everything reminded me of Jen. Gail had seen the movie, *A Walk in the Clouds*. She liked it and felt it was safe for me to see, that it wouldn't trigger any intense feelings. I was doing fine until the point in the movie where a young soldier in uniform gives his medals to his girlfriend. I burst into tears as I immediately flashed back to the moment at the mortuary where I was presented Jen's Honor Graduate medal.

Gail grabbed my hand, apologizing profusely for forgetting that part. I sobbed all the way to my car and all the way home. I walked into my office, put my head on my desk, and continued sobbing. A little voice inside me kept saying, "Look at the window." When I finally looked up, I saw Kitty sitting on the window ledge, which had to be at least four feet from the ground. She was looking directly at me.

There were several more instances where I would be talking with someone about Jen, and Kitty would appear on the window ledge of room we were in. I began to tell people to expect her. On one particular day, my friend Linda and I were sitting in my screened-in porch, having an emotional conversation about Jen. I said through my tears, "I wouldn't be surprised if Kitty showed up." Within minutes, the kitten walked onto the deck and sat there looking at us.

That evening, like every other evening, I was missing Jennifer terribly. I asked her for a sign, a message. I had a small bag that contained "Angel Cards," which are tiny slips of paper with one word on each of them. Every card has a different picture of an angel next to the word.

I reached into the bag with my eyes closed, and asked Jen to guide my hand. I pulled out a card that said "Tenderness." The angel was with a cat! Once again, I was profoundly moved. I was sure this was a message from Jen—a message to be tender with myself, to stop berating and blaming myself for her death.

The next day when Diane stopped by, I showed her the card. She looked through the entire bag and did not find another one with a cat on it. My family and friends were as convinced as I was that Jen had something to do with Kitty.

When I showed the card to my friend Joyce, she said, "Jen may have sent the kitten to give you something to nurture. Besides, you need to be tender with yourself. Jennifer's death was not your fault." She took the angel card and taped it to my refrigerator as a reminder.

Jen's car arrived from Washington about three weeks after her passing. A friend picked it up at the loading ramp and drove it to my house. I can't describe the pain in my heart when I saw her white Escort pull up.

I remembered when we bought the car together in Texas for her eighteenth birthday. I made the down payment and cosigned on the loan so she would get a better interest rate. Now, it had come home without her.

Every time I looked at her Escort sitting in the driveway, I felt an arrow piercing my heart. I wanted to take it to my local auto dealer and sell it for what we owed. I knew I could get more money if I sold it myself, but I did not want to repeatedly answer the question, "Why are you selling it?" Her father said he would be willing to handle the sale and agreed to use his phone number as the contact number.

We decided to advertise the car in a local magazine that includes pictures of the vehicles for sale. A man from the magazine came out to take the pictures. As he approached Jen's car, the kitten started hissing and whining. I knelt down next to her and, choking back tears, I said softly to her, "I don't want to sell it either, but we have no choice." Kitty then settled down. There was no doubt in my mind there was a connection between Jen and Kitty.

One evening, as we were sitting on the front step watching Kitty, Joyce, a cat owner herself, said, "I have never seen a cat behave this way.

In fact, it has been a long time since I've seen God work this way. Don't be surprised if Kitty goes away when you go back to work. She knows you can't keep her because of your travel. She's only here to help you heal."

Joyce was right. Even though my neighbor put food and water out for Kitty every day, when I returned from my first week back on the road, she was nowhere to be found.

Months later, I was talking on the phone with Joyce. She asked me if I ever saw Kitty again. I sadly said no, I hadn't but I would like to. After I hung up the phone, I took my cup of coffee and sat down on the back porch. I glanced at the back yard and almost chocked on the coffee. Kitty was looking right at me. She was bigger, but then it had been eight months since I had seen her. I opened the door to go outside, and before I could round the corner of the house she was gone. It was as if she or Jen just wanted to remind me she was still there, and she knew when I was thinking about her.

Remnants of Jen's Life

*While the words of the prophets
and the assistance of grace are available,
the journey must still be traveled alone.*

~ M. Scott Peck, M.D., *The Road Less Traveled*

The day Jenny died I was in Detroit attending a "Train-the-Trainer" session on a new product course I would be presenting. My work as a self-employed trainer was primarily with Ford Motor Company. They kept me very busy and I had little time for television or radio commercials. In addition, I was one of the lead on-camera trainers for classes broadcast over satellite television from the Detroit area. Sales consultants and managers could attend courses in dealerships anywhere in North America by turning on their television set and logging into a system that allows live, real-time interactivity. I had become a bit of a TV celebrity among Ford dealership and corporate employees.

When Jen died, I told Burt, my main contact with Ford, that I initially needed at least three weeks of bereavement leave. After that, I would assess if I was ready and able to come back. I suggested he schedule an additional trainer for my courses the first week I was due back in the event I was not ready to return. And even if I did come back, I told him it might be wise to have someone there in case I needed him or her to take over.

For my first week back at work, I was scheduled to teach two days of new product courses in Springfield, Missouri, and Wichita, Kansas. Toward the end of my third week at home, I sat down and looked at the material. I couldn't concentrate. I kept reading the first part of the course information over and over. Nothing was sinking in. I was running out of time to prepare. I felt panicked and overwhelmed. I didn't see how I could teach so soon after Jen's death.

In addition to being in the grips of profound grief, I was in the middle of taking care of my daughter's affairs. I needed to close bank accounts and cancel credit cards. I was also dealing with military issues, including the transfer home of her belongings. It looked as though they may be shipped the following week. I wanted and needed to be home to receive them.

I called Burt and told him I wasn't ready to come back.

"You *have* to teach the courses," he responded. "I don't have anyone else to send."

"What about the other trainer I suggested you pair with me?"

"She is only assigned with you the first day. There is no one available to teach the second day." He seemed to display no empathy.

I got off the phone and cried. How could I stand in front of a group of salespeople and be upbeat and enthusiastic? How could I remember horsepower ratings and rear axle ratios when I couldn't even remember my own name? And how could a child, whose mother is a motivational speaker and trainer, commit suicide?

I felt like a fraud, a phony, a failure. I tried to help numerous people become successful with sales or management techniques, but I couldn't even help my own daughter. It would be like an open-heart surgeon who devotes her life to saving people with heart disease, only to lose her own daughter to a cardiac abnormality. What a sham, a travesty.

Given no alternative, the following week I flew into Springfield. It was late and I was sitting on a wooden fence in front of the airport waiting for the hotel shuttle bus. I was talking to Jen in my head. *Jen, I don't know what goes on over there. If my talking to you keeps you here, and prevents you from moving on, then you go on. I'll be okay.* Little did I know she would answer that question the following October.

Karen, the trainer Burt paired me with in Springfield, was wonderful. She just recently joined the training team and had oriented with me for several courses. It was now her turn to help me. She set up everything, took care of all the details, and taught the morning class. I led the afternoon session, with her sitting close by if I needed her. Somehow, I got through it. It was as if I kicked into automatic pilot.

At the end of the day I caught a flight to Wichita, and Karen went on to some other city. I managed to make it through the Wichita courses, but I knew I couldn't face the following week.

I was scheduled to do four days of training in California, in a different city each day. It required two sessions a day, then getting into the focus car and driving, in some cases, several hundred miles to the next city. Driving the focus car for the training was part of my responsibility. I would then have to set up the classroom for the following day, and try to get some sleep, not to mention fitting a meal in somewhere. It was a grueling schedule for the healthiest of us, much less for someone in mourning.

Every cell in my body ached. I was exhausted just trying to live through a "normal day," much less a schedule like this one. I read in an article that one hour of grief has the physical equivalent on the body as eight hours of hard physical labor. I was a walking testimonial.

I asked Karen, when we were together, if she was scheduled for any courses the following week. She wasn't, so I asked her if she was interested in taking my week in California, given Burt's approval. She said yes, that she was happy to have the work.

I called Burt and told him I didn't think I could do the following week.

"You have to. I don't think I have anyone else."

"What about Karen?"

"I might need her for something else."

I wasn't buying that. Typically, on a Friday before the following week, trainers were being canceled. It was unusual to have work added at the last minute. *He just doesn't want to be bothered,* I thought. "Burt, you're not hearing me. I am not ready to come back to work. I tried to tell you that before the Springfield trip."

"I'll see what I could do," he relented.

He called back the next day and told me he was able to replace me for that week (with Karen). I had bought more time.

The following week, Jen's belongings were shipped home from the military. I stood alone in the garage weeping as two men unloaded 30 boxes of her things. Everything came back except Jen.

I couldn't bear to open them, yet I knew I had to find the box with her personal files. I needed to close out her bank accounts and cancel her credit cards. There was an inventory list, but for security reasons, those particular items were not listed. I silently asked for "guidance" to locate the box they were in. The first one I opened contained the paperwork I was looking for. I was spared having to look into any of the other boxes at this time. I was not ready to face that.

I sobbed as I pulled out her wallet, with her picture on her driver's license looking back at me. I felt like I was going into sacred territory. Would I find hints—bits and pieces of her life, her last moments?

The next day, I began the grueling task of making the first of many calls to various institutions, such as banks, having to speak the unspeakable over and over again: "My daughter, Jennifer Merrihew, passed away .... "

– 8 –

Letters from Boot Camp

Read me, do not let me die!
Search the fading letters, finding
steadfast in the broken binding
all that once was I.

~ Edna St. Vincent Millay, *The Poet and His Book*

Going through Jen's boxes was a very difficult and emotional task. Each box had its own story to tell. Upon opening a box with her clothing, I picked up a shirt and held it to my nose to see if I could smell her scent. Not much of her essence was there, and it was mixed with the other smells of cardboard and cigarette smoke. Some of the items needed laundering, and so, I washed my Jenny's clothes for the final time.

During one of these painful sortings, I found her black military shoes. Jennifer and I wore the same shoe size, so I put them on. Immediately, the lyrics of *our* song popped into my head. From the time she was about three years old, Jen and I used to sing to each other a line from an old Barry Manilow song, "I don't want to walk without you .... " Instead of the word "baby," I would sing "Jenny," and she would simultaneously say "Mommy." Since I was a single mom and she an only child, it became our pledge to each other—our lifeline of support through some difficult years.

Gazing at the shoes I thought, *Oh, Jen ... I don't know if I can walk without you. Maybe if I wear your shoes, particularly on days when I need to feel you close to me, this might be a way we could continue to "walk together."*

I came across a bundle of letters enclosed in a plastic bag for protection. I opened the bag and found letters I wrote to her while she was at boot camp and throughout the time she was in the service. She saved every one of them. There were 29 cards, letters, and postcards just during the three months she was at Parris Island. We weren't allowed to talk with or see each other during that time, so writing was our only means of communication.

I, too, saved every card and letter she had given to me, including the little notes she scribbled to me from the time she first began to print. I saved many of her school papers and a number of the pictures she had drawn. I had scrapbooks, boxes, and albums that were full. How glad I was I saved all of them.

As I continued to look through her boxes, I found she, too, saved everything I had ever sent.

I retrieved the box where I stored her letters to me from boot camp. I put both her letters to me and mine to her in order by dates. I wanted to recreate the feeling of having once again received her letters and to have responded to them. I sat down and began to read the first letter I sent to her:

April 27, 1994

Dear Jen,

I'm on my way to Hawaii. This is the first chance I've had to write. I was glad to hear you arrived safely. I got a message from a Ham radio operator a few days ago. Yesterday I received the postcard with your address sent by the Red Cross. Diane said she got a letter, which she said she would share with me. We're on two separate flights. Do you believe that? She flew out of Toledo and I out of Detroit. As you know, Diane won this vacation through work and was allowed to take one person along. I'm the lucky one. But the people she works for messed up the airline tickets.

I'm anxious to hear all about boot camp. I am so proud of you! I admire your courage and your strength. Always remember you have everything you need to do anything you set your mind to. Just keep focused on your goals, and go with the flow—even when you don't understand it. So many parents I've talked with are jealous. They would like to see their sons or daughters join the military. It will be a valuable experience for you—and who knows where it could lead. Just remember every morning to ask God to surround you with His white light of protection and say, "I am Divinely protected and guided, and my way is made smooth and clear." All you have to do is ask.

I've already booked a room at the Holiday Inn in Beaufort for your graduation. I also rented a car. It looks like you can come home for ten days after graduation. Let me know if you need any help booking the flight. I'd be glad to help with expenses.

Diane and I will be staying on the "Big Island" of Hawaii. It is the largest island in the chain. From Diane's description, the hotel sounds beautiful.

Keep in touch. I love you and once again, I am so proud of you. Be proud of yourself.

Love,
Mom

♦ ♦ ♦

94/04/25 (Jen's first letter to me)

Mom,

I swear I've been dying to write you ever since I got to 4th Battalion, but there has been no time. Everything is going along pretty well. Today was our last day to get ready for the real training. Tomorrow is Training Day 1 or T-day 1. Tomorrow all the physical stuff begins. I did pretty well on my Initial Strength Test. I improved all my scores. The days go by pretty fast and the meals are good (even though I'm a "weight recruit" and can't get anything in the pastry department). I guess you could say I'm enjoying myself, if anyone could really enjoy boot camp.

It's hard to explain everything that has happened so far, but I am keeping it all in my journal so I'll fill you in on all the juicy details when I get home. All I can tell you is it's crazy.

Would you please send me some "Skin so soft" body lotion? The sand fleas hate that stuff (and let me tell you they are horrible. I look like I have poison ivy and it feels just as bad.) We aren't allowed to swat or scratch, so preventative measures are in order. Thanks so much.

Things have been very stressful ever since we got to 4th BN. Life is crazy and hectic. Most of it hasn't really sunk in yet. The Drill Instructors (DI's) are very tough. In fact, they are yelling now. We aren't allowed to talk except in the line of duty. So, it's hard to make friends but I've managed. My bunkee is great. We started IPT today, which is incentive physical training. HA! If you do something wrong you do about ten different exercises at warp speed always changing.

I was doing great for a while, but today I closed the hatch (door) just as a Gun Sgt. was coming around the corner and I got busted.

All day everyone had been panting and crying after IPT and when I went up there, I thought I might die; but when I was done, everyone else was crying and hyperventilating and I wasn't even tired or breathing heavy for that matter.

How are things at home? I miss everyone. I could really use some letters if you have time. Please call Dad. Tell him I love him and to write soon. Six minutes to "Taps" ... gotta go!

Love you tons!
Jen

♦ ♦ ♦

May 8, 1994, Mother's Day (card/letter 4)

Dear Jen,

Thanks for the Mother's Day cards. I waited until today to open them. It was nice to have your letter waiting for me when I got back in town. I've enclosed the things you asked for. Let me know which you like best—the "Skin so Soft" in the bottle or in the packets.

I'm off to Houston for two weeks to conduct training. I talked with Ben today. He called to wish me a happy Mother's Day. He said he got his dad an early Father's Day gift—a kitten.

Congrats on improving your scores on your strength test. I'm proud of your courage. You can do it!

Love,
Mom

♦ ♦ ♦

94/05/08 (Jen's Letter 2)

Mother,

Happy Mother's Day. Thank you for all the letters and postcards. Every piece of mail I receive I cherish. I also want to thank you for sending out the Mother's Day cards for me [to her aunts.] That was a great help. I want to wish you a Happy Mother's Day. You deserve it. I know I haven't always been the greatest daughter, but I have always loved you and always will. And I have all the respect in the world for you.

I am so proud of all the things you've accomplished in your life and all the things you have yet to accomplish. Don't let anyone hold you back.

Give my regards to everyone back home. Send me a long descriptive letter about you and Diane in Hawaii. I am so jealous, although Boot Camp is close to Paradise! Yeah, right! Tell Diane I said, "Hello."

Things have been crazy here ... a ton of ups and downs. The whole thing is a crazy emotional rollercoaster. If the mornings go well, the afternoons suck. The evenings are almost always good and relaxing. I am always dead tired. I used to be able to study in the racks at night, but now I fall asleep before "Taps." I am sick of ironing. We have to iron our uniforms every night on our free time.

We had our first inspection yesterday. It went pretty well. Half passed—half failed. I wasn't one of the lucky ones though. Everything I did was perfect except one thing—a button in the back of my uniform was unbuttoned. Automatic failure! I almost died. I was so disappointed. Our cami uniforms have about a million pockets. We get a second chance tomorrow.

I gained a pound this week, but I lost four last week. The DI's are on my butt to lose weight because they hate my replacement for guide. [Jen was acting guide for the platoon.]

Well, I have to go to church so I'll try to write again soon. Please call Dad for me, and please send me some envelopes and stamps if you can.

Love ya,
Jen

As always, when she mentioned her dad, I would give him a call and make a copy of the letter and send it to him.

◆ ◆ ◆

May 18, 1994 (card/letter 8)

On the outside of the card is written:
"Some days it's tougher to hang in there than others!"
Inside: "Like the days you wear a really old bra with worn elastic."

Dear Jen,

I hope you're *hanging in there* okay. I'm on the road right now, and I'm looking forward to going home tomorrow to see if I got a letter from you to hear how you're doing. I thought you'd like to see the enclosed article about *Beauty and the Beast* getting nine Tony nominations. [Jen & I had seen the world debut in Houston.] It's neat to know we saw an award-winning production and performance.

I've been gone for almost a month, with only two days at home between Hawaii and Houston. Next week is Dallas/ Ft. Worth, then the week after I'll be in Detroit. I'll be going to California to be trained on the equipment used for the interactive satellite training I'll be doing for Ford. I was chosen as their lead satellite trainer.

Keep in touch.

Love ya,
Mom

♦ ♦ ♦

94/05/15 (Jen's third letter)

Mom,

Hello! How have you been? Things are going very well. I am very motivated and having a great time. Today we went on a five-mile hump and ran through the confidence course. It was incredibly motivating. I made it through all the obstacles except one (the easiest one.) My hands were really slippery. It was cool. I am beat though.

We have classes and drill this afternoon and then evening chow. I am surprised at how fast this is going in all reality. Sundays come and go very quickly. I go to church every Sunday. It helps out a ton. On Sundays we get about two hours of free time plus the time we go to church. It's a great time to regroup.

Things have calmed down. I think the DI's like me a lot. They told me I am one of the few with integrity, physical strength, and leadership skills. They really like that. Our DI's ask my opinion in private as to how the platoon is going, etc.; it's quite an honor.

Thanks for sending me all that stuff. I really needed it. I need a few more things (which she goes on to name.)

I am so glad to hear you are coming for graduation. Please change the solution in my contact case once a month and also bring them with you so I can wear them for graduation instead of these crazy birth-control glasses we have to wear.

How is my car? I miss it so much. I find myself trying to remember how to drive it and remembering how nice it was to drive to places. I am getting tired of walking everywhere. [Jen bought a car with a manual transmission to keep the cost down, even though she had never driven one. With a few quick lessons from the fellow who sold the car, she was on her way. No fear!]

I've lost twelve pounds total. It doesn't look like it though. My physical ability is increasing greatly. My sit-ups have increased to almost double. I have been getting a lot of physical activity on my own, working out on my free time.

Next week the babies come in (the new platoon.) So, we are going to get some respect. Ooh Rah!

Gotta Go. Miss you and love you.

Jen
P.S. I need stamps!

♦ ♦ ♦

May 23, 1994 (segments from letter 9)

Dear Jen,

I'm writing this en route to Dallas. I have two days in DFW, one in Houston, and Friday I'm shooting a film for the University of Michigan in Ann Arbor, where I'll be the on-camera spokesperson ... busy week!

I got to see Ben in Houston. He is taller than me now. He appreciated your letter. I told him he could use my car when he's at his mom's this summer, as long as he takes me to the airport.

Tom and my divorce was final on May 17th. I cringed when I saw the date. I didn't want it to be on Jeanne's birthday. I didn't have to appear in court, although I was in Houston on that date conducting training. (Strange twist of fate!) I've really struggled with all of this, but the past few days I feel like I've turned a corner—a good one. Things seem to be where they're supposed to be at this point in time, like my living in Michigan and being chosen head satellite trainer. All the broadcasts will be out of Dearborn, Michigan. God does work in mysterious ways.

It's great you're respected by the DI's. I'm sure with your abilities and brains you would stand out. Congrats on the twelve-pound weight loss. Do you have any idea where you'll be stationed after boot camp? Are you still interested in administration/personnel?

I love you, I'm proud of you, and my prayers are always with you.

Love,
Mom

I took a break from the letters and realized that over and over again I told her repeatedly I loved her and how I was proud of her. My eyes filled with tears as I realized I **did** tell her. She **had** to know how much I loved her. Until this point, all I could remember was the one negative letter I wrote to her—and even that incident in actuality wasn't so bad. We patched things up afterwards and become even closer as a result. But since her death, I magnified it in my mind. I eventually learned virtually everyone who has lost someone to suicide has something they feel guilty about ... whether the guilt is warranted or not. For me it was the "bad" letter, which appeared to be the only one she didn't save.

I continued to read through the letters:

June 2, 1994 (Card/letter 10)

Dear Jen,

I thought you might like to see the enclosed article about a former Marine who became an English teacher and on whose life a recent movie is based.

I'm in Detroit for a training session on a new course. At the beginning of the first day, we were asked to introduce ourselves to the group and share something people might not know. I said, "I have an eighteen-year-old daughter serving in the Marine Corps." I got applause! It was for you. Two of the conference leaders, Gregg and Hal, shared with me they were Marines, both of whom served in Nam. They said they were going to write to you.

As it stands now, I'm coming in on July 7, Thursday. I arrive in Savannah at 9:20 p.m. and will drive to Beaufort. I wanted to get in sooner so I could see you during "visiting hours" but I have to work in Detroit that day. If I can get away sooner I will. I'm booked on a free ticket, so I can change it.

Will you be coming home with me or with your father?

Write soon.

Love,
Mom

♦ ♦ ♦

94/05/28 (Jen's fifth letter)

Mother,

Thank you for all that wonderful stuff. It is greatly appreciated.

I'm sorry you are hurting because of the divorce. I still believe it is the best thing though. I know you will be happy again single. I'm telling you, it's the way to go!

Well, everything here is crazy as usual. We are getting ready to fire our weapons on Monday. All week we've had classes and hours of sitting, kneeling, standing, and laying down in firing positions (dry firing) to get used to the weapon. The positions are very uncomfortable and it is very difficult to fire. I didn't think it would be this difficult. We haven't actually fired yet, so I don't know if it's really that hard. I may be an excellent shooter, you know?

There were 58 recruits in my barracks to begin with. Now there are 42. There would be 38 but we picked up four recruits who didn't qualify on the range with their platoon who went before us. If you don't qualify on the rifle range or if you fail history testing or any other graduation require-ment, you get "recycled" to the next platoon. The platoon is three weeks behind, so your graduation date moves back three weeks. It's scary to think about being recycled. You get dumped into a platoon that's already been together for five weeks or more and you have to fit in ... get used to the new DI's and their ways. I feel really sorry for the recruits.

Speaking of graduation, it's the fifteenth of July. Tell the family so everyone can come see me get the hell out of here!

Yesterday we had a class on the dress blue uniform ... it is so awe-some. If I graduate as "Guide" or if the Platoon nominates me for Molly Marine, I get a set for free. If not, I have to buy the jacket at $106! I am very excited about the whole idea of finally getting out into the fleet and having a life again.

Mom, I know I keep saying this, but I miss you a lot. I think about you all the time and I feel bad for all the shit I've done. I love you. I never meant to hurt you in any way. I apologize for all the bad times I caused between you and Tom. Even though I still think he's a jerk, you didn't get any support from me. I'm so sorry. As soon as I find out where I'm stationed, I'll let you know. Hopefully, you can teach 100 classes there so I can see you. I want us to be closer and get along. I think I've grown up a lot and I don't want to go through anymore of my life fighting you for my independence. I want to spend it enjoying your company and advice. I love you. I'm so sorry.

Well, I have to stop crying so the people who look up to me don't lose their hero (ha, ha) and the DI's don't see me as being weak.

I have a sinus infection. I've tried to fight it off as long as I could because the DI's really pick on you for going to sick call, but I did go and they confirmed I have sinusitis. They gave me some medication. I am feeling a little better.

To give you an example of how the DI's seem to respect me, the other day they said to some of the recruits, "All of you going to sick call? I am tired of this. I can tell the ones who are faking it and the ones who are really sick, like Merrihew. She's been sick for days … I've noticed it. But she's been sucking it up. The rest of you, with your swollen ankles and fingers that look perfectly normal to me, need to learn to hack it or pack it!"

That made me feel a lot better. Well, I've got to iron my camis.

I love you,
Jen

Write soon.

♦ ♦ ♦

June 6, 1994, 50th Anniversary of D-Day (Segments of letters 11 & 12)

Dear Jen,

Your letter of 5/28 was waiting for me when I got home from Detroit. I changed my flight for your graduation to July 14. I'll arrive at 2:56 p.m. into Savannah, rent a car, and come to the base. I also booked a flight for you to go home with me. I couldn't get a flight until Saturday morning at 8:10. I thought whenever you're ready to leave the base we could go down to Savannah and stay the night there. It's a cute town, especially by the waterfront. That way we'd be closer to the airport in the morning and have some fun too.

Do you have any idea where you will go after boot camp? Will you be home for ten days?

So, do you feel like Goldie Hawn in *Private Benjamin* when she's marching in the rain saying, "I want to go out to dinner! I want to see a movie!"?

How is weapons training? Is it scary?

I really appreciated the thoughts you shared in your last letter about our relationship. It sounds like you've been doing a lot of thinking. I also look forward to a time of "enjoying each other's company." You're right ... you don't have to fight me for your independence—you've got it. I appreciate your apology.

I was sorry to hear about your sinus infection. I'm glad you got on antibiotics. I understand the military's attitude of not being a "wuss." However, I'm sure they don't teach you how to take good care of yourself.

Did the Marines do anything special for D-Day?

Take care and write soon.

Love,
Mom

♦ ♦ ♦

94/06/02 (Jen's sixth letter)

Mother,

Hello my favorite female in the world. How are you doing? I just got your packaged letter. That was the greatest! I hadn't received mail lately and that made my day. You are awesome. Things are going along here. I qualified as an Expert Shooter and ended up being the Platoon's High Shooter. It is quite an honor. I get the Senior Drill Instructor's rifle badge! I tied with the rival platoon for series high shooter, so everything is good to go.

I miss you so much, but I will be home pretty soon! I can't wait to give you a hug. I am not allowed to be affectionate in uniform, so please bring me a change of clothes so I can bear-hug you to death! Mom, I miss you so much!

Let me know if you got our flights scheduled together. Thank you. I love you.

I weigh 139#. I am so excited. I know I am going to make my goal if not less! The strange thing is I don't look any different. My waist is a little trimmer, but not much. My rear has gotten smaller though.

Mom, I miss you so much! The pictures from your trip to Hawaii were awesome. I am so glad you had a good time. I can't wait to see all these cool places. Hopefully you'll be able to visit me at my stations.

We are in Mess and Maintenance week. This is when all the recruits gain weight. Luckily, I am a squad bay recruit. That means I don't go to the chow hall. I get to stay in the barracks and clean, be on rifle watch, answer phones, and run errands. It's an honor, so I've been told. I am really glad. I have gained a lot of discipline with my eating, but if I were around food all day the calories would just jump on my body! I know they would!

Well, I have to iron my camis. I love you. Write soon.

Always, your loving daughter,
Jennifer

♦ ♦ ♦

94/06/06 (Jen's seventh letter)

In the space on the envelope for the return address Jen writes: *From one highly motivated, truly dedicated, blood-sucking war machine; ready to fight, ready to kill, ready to die, but never will.*

Mother,

I'll bet you thought you'd never hear from me this much! Well, like I said, I've done a lot of growing up.

Thank you for keeping the letters coming, especially that Memorial Day package! It couldn't have come at a better time.

A recruit got a card I think you would like:

> *"Dream your own dream and follow your own star.*
> *There wouldn't be a heaven full of stars*
> *If we were all meant to wish on the same one.*
> *There will always be dreams grander and humbler*
> *than your own,*
> *But there will never be a dream exactly like your own.*
> *For you are unique and more wondrous than you know.*
> *Do your best.*
> *There are no shortcuts on the way to a dream.*
> *So, give all that you have to all that you do,*
> *And above all things, believe in yourself.*
> *This is all the dream asks of you,*
> *But it is everything!"*

I thought that was an awesome card.

Thanks for the article on the Marine schoolteacher. You must have been reading my mind because I have been thinking a lot about teaching lately. I am trying to figure out what classes to take while in the M.C. to help me when I get out. The M.C. has programs, study courses called MCI (Marine Corps Institute). You go to the education office at your base and request the class you want to take. They give you the materials, a deadline, and a date to take your final exam. You teach yourself, take the exam, and get college credits. And it's FREE! Isn't that awesome?

I have to be disciplined enough to take the time to do it. I will! So much of me has changed. You'll be amazed.

Well, I'm going blind from writing in the racks. I love you! Send all my love to the family.

Write soon,
Jennifer

By the way, has Tristin called?

◆ ◆ ◆

94/06/12 (Jen's tenth letter)

Mom,

It makes me feel closer to you when I am writing to you.

Well, Mess & Maintenance ends today. We turned in our camis to get name stamps on them. I am so excited and very motivated. The recruits really care about me, and that makes me feel so good. Every morning this week, I've had the 0300-0500 rifle watch, so I've gotten the chance to wake everyone up and send them off to work in the morning. Today I had the late shift, but I got up anyway to say good morning and answer questions. Everyone really seems to appreciate me. They all come to me with their problems, and I try to help them the best I can. It feels really good. I do little things for them around the squad bay, and they in turn make sure I get Raisin Bran at every meal at the chow hall. It sounds silly, but if there is no Raisin Bran, they will find some from somewhere for me. Isn't that cool? It makes life easier here to know they care.

I completely forgot Father's Day was in June, so I didn't get Dad a card before I left for boot camp. I hope he'll accept a make-shift card from here. Do you think he will?

About your outfit … graduation will be outside as long as it doesn't rain (and it rains a lot here, so be prepared.) It is very humid, muggy, and hot here, so wear something loose and cool, but semi-dressy. You can pretty much wear whatever you want, but look nice (not that you don't always.)

(This was a long letter and she talks about the mail she's received and her favorite packages and letters. She closes with …)

Boot camp has been so awesome for me in a growing way, as you can probably tell from my letters. Did you get my apology letter? Do you accept my apology? I truly meant everything I said. I love you so much. I've learned the importance of family and teamwork … helping people out. I know a lot of things I never realized before. Things that are too hard to explain, but you'll see it. I've learned discipline and how to eat right. I am a very healthy eater now. Everything I've learned is important and has made me who I am now. I am really proud of myself.

Do you think we could have a get-together at the house Saturday night? I really want to see everyone together. That would be nice to have a party (with cake ... hint! hint!) This is really important and I want to celebrate. I'll do all the errands because the first thing I want to do is drive my car!

I think the most important thing about Boot Camp is I've found myself. I've found my strengths and my weaknesses, my fears and everything I want to be. I want to learn and be the best at everything I do. Not the best as in #1, but the best as in the best of my ability.

I love you. Write soon!

Always,
Jennifer

◆ ◆ ◆

94/06/09 (Jen's eleventh letter)

Mom,

I keep bombarding you with letters, but it's hard to be away from you, and writing makes me feel like I am talking to you.

I lost one of my best friends today. She didn't qualify on the Range. We lost a total of six recruits because of the rifle Range! I can't believe how many recruits this Platoon has lost—a total of 27! We had 62, now we have 35. Three of them were really good recruits too. Recruit Rowe was one of my closest friends here. Well, I guess I'll see her in the chow hall some time. It was awful, especially since the beginning was so rough. The whole platoon cried last night; it was very moving.

I am doing very well myself. I am getting in the right frame of mind for graduation and the real fleet. You will be so impressed with me. I am so different. I have no breasts anymore! I probably wear a size AA by now, if not a training bra.

Anyway, thank you again for all the support you've always given me ... especially in those hard times. There are girls here who just got their wisdom teeth pulled and they have to eat chow with us. They can't have their moms bring them soup, ice cream, and Fruit Roll-ups as you did for me! You are definitely the greatest.

Have you heard from Ben? I still haven't heard a word, and I don't know if he is in Ohio or in Texas.

Tell Grammies I said hello and I love her. The next few weeks we are going to the field, so I won't be able to write. We leave on Thursday the 16th, so when you don't hear from me, don't worry. Please pass the word around that I'm sorry I don't have time to write to everyone, but I miss them and am doing fine. Keep the letters coming.

Love you,
Jennifer

◆ ◆ ◆

She actually did write to me from the field. I sent her self-addressed stamped envelopes, and she used those during that time. I also think this is when she put all the letters I wrote to her in a plastic Ziploc bag so they wouldn't get ruined. She must have taken them with her. I continued reading through the rest of our letters together during her stay on Parris Island. Then I began reading the ones I wrote to her when she was stationed at Headquarters Marine Corps in Arlington, Virginia.

Eventually, I came to a letter I wrote to her in January 1995, shortly after she came home for a respite and had returned to the base. It was one of the first letters I wrote to her after the "bad" letter. She was having significant problems with Sgt. Wesson and Dick at HMC and was very upset.

January 31, 1995

Dear Jen,

"Life is a grindstone. Whether you get ground down or polished up depends on what you are made of." (I go on to talk about some of the issues she is dealing with and say ....) There are some things you can do that might help you get through this. Get to the gym and work out—it's a great stress reducer. Throw some punches into the punching bag. Get your anger out; don't turn it inward on yourself. That's how depression results.

Get off base and do things. Check out the Metro. Find the library and the Mall. Go see the Smithsonian museums. Go to the National Archives. See the Constitution and what rights and privileges you have. You are in an exciting place right now. Reach out and invite others to join you, but choose your company carefully.

Focus on your work. Keep your personal life out of the office. I know this is extremely hard on you, but you have such an exciting opportunity. Try not to generalize your anger toward everyone and everything. Each person, each situation should be treated separately.

I've been thinking about how both you and I are in male-dominated occupations. It's no coincidence you are where you are. God has plans for you. It was no mistake you were the Honor Grad. It takes a special woman to not only survive in that environment, but to excel. You have an opportunity to make a difference. Women all over the world are starting to make a difference, from Congress to the military to the automotive industry.

Concentrate on your schooling. It's your future. If you want to get back at anyone, do it by succeeding. Continue your writing. Some of the greatest songs, poems, and stories are written when people are going through tragedy and loss. Keep a journal; it helps to sort things out.

Take care of yourself. Eat right and exercise. To survive this, you need to be healthy and have the strength to go forth. The right people and jobs just can't help to be attracted to a successful person who has her act together. Do your inner work. Follow through with your idea to volunteer in a day care, or a children's wing of a hospital.

Take control of your mind and thinking; don't let it control you. Get a *Walkman* with earphones and listen to your positive affirmation tapes every night. Surround yourself with white light and ask for God's protection each day as soon as you wake up. Thank your guardian angels for their protection. Pray. Most of all, remember you are loved!

Well, this sounds like a Robert Fulghum novel, *Everything I Needed to Know I Learned in Kindergarten*. Remember, there are so many people who love you. Don't waste any more time with people who are incapable of love.

You can come home as much as you want. You can get through this! Call anytime. I love you.

Love,
Mom

♦ ♦ ♦

Little did I know when I wrote that letter that ten months later I would be thrust into circumstances where I would, once again, need to follow my own advice. Losing Jennifer was the ultimate test of survival ... would I make it?

Finding all those letters helped to remind me of some of the positive things I said and did for Jennifer. Her suicide left me feeling like such a failure.

-9-

Smile, Though Your Heart Is Aching

You must do the thing which you think you cannot do.

~ Eleanor Roosevelt

As I gradually merged back into the work force, the end of the business day became a very difficult time for me, particularly if I had been conducting a training course. I would be distracted, somewhat, from my grief during the course. And, as all trainers know, there's a bit of a "high" when one is in front of a group if it's going well. The adrenaline is flowing, and often the audience or class is providing positive feedback and energy.

Coming off of those moments, and realizing over and over again I had to go home to an empty house or hotel room, and face a life without Jen, was excruciatingly painful.

I experienced the same "punch in the stomach" I felt every morning upon awakening. But now, it slugged me again around five o'clock each day as well. There was no hanging around at the end of the day, lapping up the positive strokes or conversing with colleagues. I had only a short time to get to my car, once reality hit, before I would crumble. Getting through a workday was like trying to keep a lid on a steaming teakettle. One had to release the pressure at some point. Holding all the grief in until five o'clock each day was about all I could handle. When I was alone in my car the dam seemed to break and the tears flowed—sometimes so profusely I could barely see to drive.

Airplanes were another place where the grief seemed to pour out, and it was much more embarrassing. I would take a window seat and pretend to look out, all the while blowing my nose and wiping my eyes. I resorted to carrying cloth handkerchiefs with me, since I couldn't carry enough tissues to handle the job. I took the large white handkerchiefs that were military issue for Jen. What a bitter irony I would be the one using them.

Traveling became extremely difficult for me. I'm not exactly sure why. Maybe it was because, when I was on the road, I was away from my support systems. Being in strange cities and hotels seemed to intensify my loneliness and despair. In addition, when I was away from home, I was always with people who didn't know my situation. The ongoing charade of seeming to appear and act normal was taking its toll.

I began to wish our culture continued the custom of wearing black for a year after a death. At least that would help explain to people why I seemed distracted at times, why I stumbled over words, and why I choked every time someone innocently asked me about my family.

I dreaded meeting anyone new, for fear they would ask me the question that had the power to bring me to my knees—"Do you have any children?" How was I supposed to answer that? I would stumble and stutter and fight back tears. Sometimes I would say no, depending on the circumstances. If I was in a training session and couldn't afford to fall apart, saying I didn't have any children seemed to be the best way to handle it. At other times, I would answer "No" in order to spare the inquiring person the discomfort of having accidentally stumbled onto a sensitive and painful subject.

At the same time I was teaching seminar-based courses in the field for Ford, I was also conducting a number of distance learning courses on a satellite television network for Ford. I had been chosen as the lead satellite trainer for Ford and provided the training for their very first satellite broadcast. I helped to train other satellite trainers.

I was in the middle of preparing for a new satellite program when Jen died. I was scheduled to present the new satellite course the following week.

The company recently put a trainer evaluation protocol in place, which was to be utilized the first time a trainer presented a new course. Given the considerable number of satellite courses I taught in the past, it was surprising I was never formally evaluated. Any one of those programs would have been a great one to evaluate. But Burt scheduled me for an evaluation during my first satellite program following Jen's death, and on a course I had never presented before. I asked him if he would postpone the evaluation, given my circumstances. I certainly did not need that added pressure. Besides, it may not accurately reflect the type of work I normally do. He was not willing to reconsider his decision. He quoted policy to me and the discussion was closed.

A few days prior to the broadcast Cheri, the trainer coach who was to evaluate me, sat down with me to go over my goals and objectives for this program. She was aware of my situation. When she asked me what my goals were, I looked at her and simply said, "To get through it." That was the end of the conversation.

The four days of broadcasts went well. At the end of the first day, Cheri came in the studio with tears in her eyes. She said to me, "I don't know how you accomplished what you just did. You did an excellent job. You kept the program moving, you used humor, and you created a great rapport with your audience. I could sense love coming from you to the participants."

I was amazed with Cheri's last comment. How did she know that's what I was doing? I never told anyone that before I present a class or broadcast, I say a prayer asking God to bless and prosper all who are in attendance. It was unusual for a trainer to say something like that, but Cheri was a pleasant exception. I found it interesting she was the one scheduled to be with me—someone who was sensitive, compassionate, and spiritual, and I might add, given the male-dominated profession, a woman. Likewise, it was Karen and not one of the guys who was paired with me in Springfield. Karen and I were the only seminar-based female trainers among a core of approximately forty.

At the end of the four days, Cheri was required to fill out a written evaluation. In it she said:

> Overall, Joyce did an outstanding job. Her delivery was smooth, controlled, and consummately professional. She is a credit to the team and a role model for other trainers aspiring to achieve excellence. (She went on to compliment specific skills and said,) Considering the context in which Joyce delivered this first broadcast, I watched her performance with awe and reverence. When asked what her goals were for the course, she responded not surprisingly, 'To get through it.' Joyce gave 100% of her-self—heart and mind—to her students. She successfully put their needs first and rose to a level of professionalism that dem-onstrates the quality of her character and strength of her spirit.
>
> Few trainers are capable of bringing personal excellence and commitment to their profession. Joyce is to be commended for showing all of us what it means to be our best.

I will keep that evaluation forever as a reminder we **can** do what we think we can't, and what may look like a problem or obstacle may actually be an opportunity in disguise. Nonetheless, it was extremely difficult to be upbeat and enthusiastic when my whole world had fallen apart. How long could I keep this up?

What Would Og Tell Me to Do?

We had to teach the despairing men,
that it did not really matter what we expected from life,
but rather what life expected from us.

~ Viktor Frankl, *Man's Search for Meaning*

In late October, just a few weeks after Jennifer died, I got a call from Phil, an associate who worked in the education department of Ford Motor Company. Ford had recently launched a pilot for a large-scale leadership program and was in the process of hiring trainers. Phil knew my long-term goal was to move from product-specific training to leadership training. He knew of my training skills and liked my style. He called to tell me the pilot programs went well and asked if I was interested in joining the team. He also knew of my circumstances.

"I don't think I should make any changes right now," I told him.

"I understand," he said. "However, this is slated to only be a two-year project, and if you don't come on board now, you may not have the chance later. We are in the process of conducting interviews at this time."

"Who do I need to see?"

He gave me the necessary information and contact people. I took the information, not knowing what I would do with it. I read in grief books it is better not to make significant changes early in the mourning process. I thought it was sound advice. But here was a project I wanted to be a part of for some time. The opportunity couldn't have come at a worse time for me personally.

A different team than the one I was working with headed up the leadership program. Even though I was an independent contractor, I knew I would need to get Burt's permission to interview for a position. Burt had a long history of being territorial with "his" trainers, in spite of the fact we were all independent contractors. He blocked opportunities for employment outside of his projects, even though they were within Ford Motor Company. This also happened during times we were not getting much work with his projects. I knew approaching him with my desire to facilitate the leadership program would be no easy task.

When I first came back to work, I discussed with Burt briefly my desire to not travel as much at this time. I asked to be scheduled primarily for the distance learning courses, which were broadcast from Detroit. Once again, he seemed totally unsympathetic toward my situation. He told me he was not going to treat me any differently than the rest of his trainers. Traveling was part of the job, he reiterated.

I long sensed that he did not like female trainers. After all, it was a male-dominated profession. He was not the one to hire me. He co-managed the department with John.

I scheduled an appointment to talk with Burt about the leadership program. I wasn't sure if I could make a change right now, but I also wasn't thrilled about continuing to associate with someone who seemed so unwilling to work with my requests during this difficult time.

I was beside myself. I certainly didn't need additional challenges at this point. I was so emotionally raw and vulnerable. I prayed to God for direction, guidance, and strength.

The meeting with Burt started with discussing contract negotiations for next year. I was on a yearly contract, and there were only two months left on the current one. He said the budget was tight and there would be essentially no raise for next year. I knew the leadership program was paying their trainers significantly more.

It was time to bring up the new project. I don't know where my initial words came from. "Burt, do you believe in God?"

He looked surprised by the question but replied, "Yes."

"I do as well. I also believe He has a purpose for each one of us. I feel my next step professionally is to do more in the way of motivational and inspirational training, the type of training that makes a broader difference in people's lives. I thought I would have to leave the automotive industry to achieve this, until I heard about the leadership program. It seems to match my goals. I'd like the opportunity to interview for a facilitator position. If I'm accepted, I'd be willing to help train others to teach my current courses. I'm not sure how many weeks per month the leadership program would need me. If it's not full time, I'd be happy to continue teaching the satellite and field courses."

I could see he wasn't pleased with my announcement, and I wasn't surprised by his reaction. He shook his head, saying, "I need you full time and I'm not willing to share you. Besides, the leadership program is only slated to be a two-year program. If you decide to become involved with that program, you'll never work for me again. Even if you did work for that program, you would continue to be paid at the same salary rate."

I knew that was not the case. The additional money wasn't my primary motivation. The greatest draw for me was the program offered the type of training I had been working toward. I wanted to move away from product-specific training. But rather than being confrontational, I decided to use the "Columbo" approach of asking questions to get at the truth.

"I'm a little confused, Burt. Do the leadership trainers report to you?

"No," he responded reluctantly.

I knew I had cornered him. "I don't understand then, why my salary would be frozen if I moved to that project."

He continued to be argumentative. Finally, I looked at him and said, "All I'm asking is that I have an opportunity to interview. Are you willing to give the okay to the people who are doing the interviews?" I heard they had been given explicit instructions from him not to interview any of "his" trainers.

He relented and said, "Yes."

I should have stayed around and listened to him make the call. I found out later he threw a lot of barriers in my path. I didn't understand why the woman who was coordinating the interviews wouldn't return my calls, especially since they were in such a hurry to hire trainers. It soon became clear Burt told her just enough that she considered me a "hot potato," and didn't want to touch me. Even though my contract with him ended in December, he had taken the liberty of scheduling me for his programs through March.

The leadership program needed trainers to begin in January. He told the woman in charge of hiring I wouldn't be available until after March. He also told her I would have to be hired at the same salary I was currently being paid. Furthermore, he told her I was "just an RN" and I didn't have the background they were looking for, even though I had management and organizational development experience in healthcare.

He could have simply told the truth—that he considered me one of his top trainers and didn't want to lose me. I was requested often throughout the United States for the various courses I taught. I was also one of the lead trainers on satellite.

It took some intervention from Phil with the woman's boss to grant me an interview. I wondered if any of this was worth the trouble, given there was so much other horror in my life. I barely had the energy to get through a day, much less doing battle with Burt.

I thought back to my plans and goals before Jen died. I remembered a specific incident that occurred around the time I first considered shifting my focus to motivational and inspirational training.

In mid-1993, I had just finished reading *The Return of the Ragpicker*, by Og Mandino. The messages in Og's books, such as *The Greatest Miracle in the World*, were a tremendous inspiration to me, as was Og himself. His personal story of transformation from an alcoholic on the verge of suicide, to a motivational speaker and author continued to influence my life.

Upon finishing *Return of the Ragpicker*, I remember thinking, *what would Og tell me to do as my next step in becoming a motivational speaker?* I tucked the question away for another day. Tom and I were in the process of separating, and I was in the throes of finding a house and moving back to the Toledo area. I had enough on my plate for the moment.

Two years later, in August of 1995, I was scheduled to conduct training in San Antonio. By that time, I was settled in my home in Michigan. I was just beginning to heal from the trauma of the divorce, which was finalized in May of 1994. Jen had been in the Corps approximately a year-and-a-half. I was once again starting to entertain thoughts of doing more in the area of motivational and inspirational speaking.

I had recently purchased Og Mandino's latest book, *The Spellbinder's Gift*. I didn't know what it was about, and I hadn't bothered to read the book jacket synopsis. It didn't matter, since I read everything Og writes. I decided to take it along to read on the plane, still having no clue as to the contents.

I finished my work in San Antonio a little earlier than expected, and took a different flight home from the one originally scheduled. I settled into my seat and opened *The Spellbinder's Gift*. Much to my amazement, it was about a motivational speaker. I was astonished to find I had unconsciously chosen to bring along a book addressing the very subject foremost in my mind.

I was well into the book when a flight attendant announced a medical emergency and asked if there were any nurses or doctors on board. Not stopping to mark my place in the book, I closed it quickly and pulled my attendant call button. I indicated I was a nurse, and the flight attendant took me to a woman who was in obvious medical distress. She was having extreme difficulty breathing and was wearing an oxygen mask.

"Are you having any chest pain?" I asked.

She gasped, "No, I ... just ... can't breathe."

Her skin was ashen gray and I couldn't feel her pulse. She appeared to be in shock. I told the flight attendant the woman's feet needed to be elevated. To do that, we needed to move her to the other side of the plane, which had three seats in the row. She was in a two-seat row.

The flight attendant began asking people to move and they were responding accordingly. I glanced back at the ailing woman and saw her eyes had rolled back in her head. I shouted to the attendant, "We have to move her immediately!" Without waiting for help, I lifted the woman across the aisle and placed her on the empty seats. I must have experienced that adrenalin rush people refer to when they lift things beyond their typical strength. I spoke loudly to the surrounding passengers saying, "Please give me as many blankets and pillows as you can."

Quickly, they obliged and I placed the pillows and blankets under the woman's feet to elevate them. She needed an increased blood supply to her brain and vital organs. I requested a medical kit, which the flight attendant quickly provided. I retrieved the blood pressure cuff and placed it on the lady's arm. I had difficulty hearing her blood pressure so I checked it by feeling her pulse. The systolic pressure was 78, when it should have been around 120. She was clearly in shock.

I began to envision a plan in the event her heart stopped beating. I would have to place her on the floor in the aisle, and kneel between the seats to do CPR. I kept my fingers on her barely perceptible pulse to continue monitoring it. She was still conscious.

"What's your name?" I asked her.

"Kathleen."

"Mine is Joyce."

There wasn't anything I could do further without the proper medical equipment and medications. I began to pray, *Dear God, there's nothing more I can do. I need help. Please help us get her to the gate.*

Suddenly her pulse began to get stronger. Her skin became warmer and drier, and her color improved. She looked at me with surprise and said, "I can breathe easier. I feel better."

"You *are* better," I told her, trying to conceal my amazement.

"We're about to land," the flight attendant informed me. "You need to be buckled in."

I lifted Kathleen's feet, sat down with her feet on my lap and the flight attendant buckled us both in with the same seat belt. There was not enough time for the flight attendant to be seated. She knelt in front of

Kathleen. We both reached out to her. Kathleen held one arm and I held the other as the plane landed in Memphis.

A medical team came on board and began to ask Kathleen questions, some of which I answered.

"Are you a friend of Kathleen's?" one of the medical team asked me.

"No, I'm just a passenger."

Kathleen looked at me and said most emphatically, "Yes, you *are* my friend."

I smiled and said, "I guess you're right." She glanced back at me with an expression of gratitude as they helped her off the plane.

I changed planes for the final leg home. Once settled, I opened my book. I had not marked my place when the flight attendant made the announcement about needing a doctor or nurse. I opened the book to a random page looking for something familiar. The first sentence I read on the page said, *My God, Horace is having a heart attack!*

I knew I hadn't gotten that far, so I ruffled back through pages until finding my spot. When I got to the page about Horace and the heart attack, I was dumbfounded. At this point in the story, the motivational speaker, around whom the book is centered, is giving his first speech arranged by his new agent. Horace, the CEO of the corporation for whom he is speaking, has just introduced him. The motivational speaker is on the stage giving his talk, when he glances down in front of him and sees Horace slumped in his chair with his eyes rolled back. He jumps off the stage, lifts the CEO, puts him on the floor and starts praying. Horace comes around.

At this point I couldn't read anymore because of the tears filling my eyes. The very same thing just happened to me moments before. I remember looking up and thinking, *When you want to get my attention, Lord, you sure know how to do it!* I had been asking for a sign, for guidance with respect to my next professional move. *What would Og tell me to do next?* He wrote an entire book about a motivational speaker!

I felt compelled to write to Mr. Mandino and tell him what transpired. Something deep inside me knew he would write back. In my letter, I told him the influence he played in my life. I shared my desire to be a motivational speaker, and my question to him after reading *The Return of the Ragpicker*. I went on to explain the events on the plane that occurred while I was reading *The Spellbinder's Gift*. At the bottom of the letter I typed, *P.S. Og, what do I do now?* I sent it to him, in care of his publisher.

Within three weeks, on September 7, he wrote back with the following:

Dear Joyce,

What a lovely letter! Many thanks for all your kind words.

Your P.S. "Og, what do I do now?" hit me. Are you ready? Join the National Speakers Association. We are a group of more than 2000 professional speakers, and the three- or four-day annual convention in July will be an experience you will never forget. (He gave me the address, adding) You won't regret it.

Have a wonderful life.

Warmest,
Og

P.S. I'll be at the Church of Today (Warren, Michigan), Second Sunday in December."

One month after receiving his letter my daughter was dead.

Keeping focused on the extraordinary set of circumstances surrounding Og's book was the only reason I kept forging ahead with my career goals, even in the face of great odds. It was as if the road markers were put in place, knowing that when the opportunity came, I would need direction, strength, and inspiration.

–11–

No Contract and No Daughter

The depth of darkness to which you can descend and still live is an exact measure of the height that you can aspire to reach.

~ Laurens van der Post

My audition and interview for the leadership program was scheduled for November 3, barely a month after Jen died. I was to present a portion of a subject familiar to me that included participant interaction. The audition would be videotaped.

How in the world could I do this? It's one thing to teach a class I was familiar with; it was another to have to prove myself in the middle of profound grief. I wasn't feeling very good about myself, or about life. I didn't even want to wake up in the morning. Who was I to try to inspire and motivate others?

My thoughts drifted to the time I auditioned for the satellite training program. It was in early May 1994. I had just moved to Michigan six weeks prior. The day before the audition, my divorce papers arrived for my signature. Their presence made it all so final and a reminder of a second marriage failure.

I woke up the morning of the audition feeling physically ill. I wondered how I would ever get through it, much less do well. I prayed all the way to Detroit. "God, if this be Your will, please give me the strength and resources to do a good job."

When I got to the interview and the camera was turned on, it was like a switch was flipped, as if something or someone took over for me. I did very well and subsequently landed the lead trainer position for the satellite distance learning project.

I tried to focus on the memory of that experience as the audition for the leadership program approached. I hoped I would be able to find the same type of strength.

The audition and interview for the leadership program were grueling. There wasn't a friendly face among the eight people present. They grilled me as if I were an enemy force to be reckoned with. I wondered how much Burt was responsible for their attitude. *My God,* I thought. *What is it going to be like to work with these people? Was there no compassion anywhere in the universe?*

Upon completion, I was told I would need to be available for a "train the trainer" session in early January. After that, I would need to audit one of the leadership seminars. Next, I would have to teach at one of the sessions. Depending on how I performed, they would let me know if I was accepted. It would be at least February—three months—before a decision would be made.

Burt wanted an answer immediately. I explained the situation, but his response was the same, "You'll need to give me an answer by the end of the week."

"I don't know if I'm accepted for the program yet."

"That's not my problem. I'm working on the second quarter for next year and I need to finish it."

I sighed and told him I would give him my decision by week's end.

After much anguish, I decided to resign from Burt's program. I didn't want to work for a man who was so rigid and insensitive. I wrote my letter of resignation and headed into the holidays without my daughter and without a signed contract for the following year.

We Don't Die

Part of the soul's continuing spiritual vocation
in the hereafter is to help their families to understand
that we are all on our own spiritual journey …
and not to get sidetracked by our loss ….

~ George Anderson & Andrew Barone, *Lessons from the Light*

The pain of Jen's passing continued to be unbearable. As Thanksgiving approached and I was facing the holidays without her, I thought, *I can't do this. I can't live like this for the rest of my life.*

I called my friend, Gail, and said to her through my sobs, "I don't think I can do this."

She knew exactly what I meant. Her immediate response was, "I'm coming over."

Gail showed up at the door with dinner. We talked, we cried, I lamented. She asked me, "Did you ever read that book, *We Don't Die?*"

We talked about this book when we vacationed together in Greece the May before Jen passed. I purchased it but never read it.

I went into my bedroom and retrieved it. Gail began to read to me like a mother comforting her child who awakened from a nightmare screaming. It was at that moment my healing journey began.

Over the next few days, I devoured the book. The author, Joel Martin, tells of the amazing ability of George Anderson to discern spirits on the "other side." Account after account describes Anderson delivering messages to people who are grieving the loss of a loved one, from the very loved ones they are grieving. The discernments revealed information that could have only come from the "person" who was sending the message. In addition, the spirit's particular personality and word choice emerged. Story after story reinforced the same message—we don't die—our spirit lives on.

That was not a new concept for me. I had been reading the literature on near-death experiences (NDE's) since the mid-seventies. Dr. Raymond Moody is considered to be the pioneer in bringing awareness of NDE's to the public. In a near-death experience, a person is *clinically* dead, that is, they have no heartbeat or respirations. They are either brought back to life by a medical team, or they come back on their own. Those who experience this phenomenon describe several similar themes, as Dr. Moody explains in his book, *The Light Beyond*:

> ... a sense of being dead, peace, and painlessness even during a "painful" experience, bodily separation, entering a dark region or tunnel, rising rapidly into the heavens, meeting deceased friends and relatives who are bathed in light, encountering a Supreme Being, reviewing one's life, and feeling reluctance to return to the world of the living.[2]

Having been a critical care nurse, I was familiar with patients who had a cardiac or respiratory arrest, and who were brought back by resuscitation. I talked with people who had experienced NDE's. When I taught critical care nursing, I thought it was important for nurses to at least be exposed to the concept and possibility. I would assign an article to be read on NDE's and then we would discuss it. I would wrap up the discussion with the comment, "Regardless of your own personal beliefs about an afterlife, or NDE's, if a patient tells you about their NDE, you can now honestly say to them that others have described similar experiences."

It was important for them to affirm the patient's experience, or he or she may not discuss it any further. The person may think he or she was going crazy if the experience wasn't validated.

After finishing *We Don't Die*, I read Martin's subsequent books about Anderson: *We Are Not Forgotten* and *Our Children Forever*. I continued to read everything I could get my hands on about NDE's, death and afterlife references. It was the only thing that brought me any semblance of comfort and hope. I would never survive this if I didn't think I would see Jen again someday.

Meredith and Michelle came to spend Thanksgiving with me. I cherished the time we spent together. Their presence helped me to get through that first Thanksgiving without Jen.

I continued teaching the rest of the sales courses on my schedule through December. I did not send out Christmas cards, or put up a tree. I couldn't bear to go into the ornament box and find all of Jen's special ornaments, like the one that said, "Baby's first Christmas" or the reindeer Jen made out of a wooden clothespin.

Needless to say, I was not in a holiday mood. I wished I could go to a place where Christmas was not celebrated and stay there until the holidays were over. Most of my nights were spent crying myself to sleep. I did find the courage to venture into the mall one day to buy a few gifts. It was extremely difficult to see the Christmas decorations and to hear the holiday music. I quickly bought what I needed and got out of there. I sent Tristin a package consisting of a Trivial Pursuit game, Pepperidge Farm Mint Milano cookies, a coffee cup. and some coffee—reflecting his favorite memories of times spent with Jen.

The one place I did want to go was to the Church of Today in Warren, Michigan to see Og Mandino. Diane agreed to go with me. Og gave a very touching speech after which he signed books. I took my copy of *The Spellbinder's Gift*, which he autographed. We talked briefly about the letters we exchanged. He shared with me he had been struggling with heart problems. I found him to be very warm and personable.

During the ride home, I thought of how significant it was Og should autograph the very book that played such a pivotal role for me. What I didn't know is that was the last time Og would ever speak at the Church of Today. He died the following September.

–13–

Someone to Watch Over Me

The worst is not that we may be overwhelmed by disaster,
but to fail to live by principle.

~ Sister Wendy Beckett, *Meditations on Peace*

One evening, a few weeks before Christmas, Meredith called. She began to tell me about a dream she had the previous night. "Yesterday I was shopping at a store called the Yankee Peddler. Later that night in a dream I was 'instructed' to return to the Yankee Peddler and buy a plaque for you, which contained a verse addressed to 'Mother.' I thought to myself in the dream, *Why would I buy a 'mother' plaque for Joyce? She's not my mother, although I think of her as a second mother.* Maybe Jen was telling me to buy this for you." Just as she finished saying that, she started to gasp.

"What's wrong?" I asked.

"As soon as I made reference to the message possibly coming from Jen, I experienced a hot feeling coursing through my body."

"Maybe it *was* a message from Jen," I responded.

The next day Meredith called me.

"Joyce, I went back to the same store to try to find the plaque I saw in my dream, but there weren't any containing the words from the dream. In fact, there was only one plaque with writing on it. The rest of them just had pictures. So, I bought the only one with words. I'll bring it when I come to your house for Christmas."

"Would you please write down the words you saw in the dream?"

"I'll try," she said. I learned later she couldn't remember them, but she didn't have the heart to tell me.

Meredith went home to her parent's house for Christmas before she came to see me. While staying there, she had another dream where the words she originally saw in the first dream came back to her. She awakened and wrote them down on a tissue box by her bed.

When she arrived at my house, she gave me the plaque. There were little angels on it and it said: "There are angels watching over you." Tears ran down my cheeks. I remembered Meredith said this was the only plaque that had words on it. Then I looked in the lower left corner of the plaque and chills ran through me. I said to Meredith, "You *did* get the right plaque!"

In the corner, was a little can with "star dust" written on it. *Star Dust* was the street we lived on in Texas. As the tears continued to flow, she handed me a piece of paper with the words she was "given" in her dream—the message from Jen: "I don't know where these words have been. You're not just my mother, you're my best friend."

No words could have meant more. It appeared I *had* gotten a Christmas gift from Jennifer after all.

Meredith stayed on through New Year's Eve. On New Year's Day I drove her to the Detroit airport. She needed to return to her Marine base in Arlington, Virginia. Her visit meant so much.

My mind hadn't been quite the same since Jen had passed. I kept forgetting little things—like checking the fuel level in my car. As I exited the freeway on my way back from the airport, I noticed my fuel gauge was on empty. I was in the country about twenty miles from home. There was nothing and no one around. I could not make it home without additional fuel.

I wondered if I would be able to find an open gas station. I pulled into the parking lot of a small convenience store with two gas pumps, the old-fashioned kind one hardly saw anymore with the rounded tops. In the past, I had driven by this store several times, but I rarely saw any customers. I never bought gas here, but I thought I would give it a try. I looked at the store and saw a sign saying "Open."

I cranked the starter lever, placed the nozzle in my tank and tried to start the gas flow. Nothing came. I cranked the starter lever on the pump a second time and tried again. Gas began flowing. I filled my tank and went to pay for the gas. The door to the store was locked. *That's odd*, I thought. *Maybe the person working here is in the back room.* I knocked loudly several times. No one answered the door. There didn't seem to be any lights on. The store must have been closed after all. *Funny they should leave the pumps on*, I thought. But I was grateful I had gas to get home.

I got back in my car and made a note of the amount I owed them. I decided I would drop the money off the next time I came by this way.

About a week later, I stopped back at the store. I told the man behind the counter I had gotten gas on New Year's Day and I was here to pay for it. With a strange look on his face he said, "We were closed on New Year's. No one was here."

I explained to him how I hadn't realized that until after I pumped the gas. "The sign on the door indicated you were open," I said.

He looked at me as if he had seen a ghost. I wasn't sure if he was more surprised by my honesty or by the fact I had gotten gas out of those pumps. Seeing the expression on his face, I asked him if the pumps still worked. I thought maybe there was a bigger mystery here than I originally realized.

"Yes, they work," he scratched his head and muttered, then looked at me resolutely and said, "but I am certain I turned them off the night before."

We stood looking at one another for a moment, both of us a bit confused. I then gave him the money, thanked him and walked out. He was still shaking his head when I drove away.

I wondered, as I drove off, if I experienced one of those miracles people talk about. Did my guardian angel or my deceased father or my daughter help somehow to turn on the pump? I have no answer. I only know I got gas from a closed gas station, out of a pump that was older than dirt and was supposed to be turned off.

-14-

New Beginnings in January

The best decision-makers are those who are willing
to suffer the most over their decisions
but still retain their ability to be decisive.

~M. Scott Peck, M.D., *The Road Less Traveled*

Somehow, I had gotten through the holidays, but I had yet to face a date that would magnify Jen's absence even more—January 12, her birthday. She would have been twenty. How would I ever get through that? What was I supposed to do with that day? A child's birthday is an intimate occasion between the mother and the child, a remembrance of a moment when I brought her into the world. Holidays are shared by everyone. Who would hold my hand through this day?

Meredith and I talked about my coming to Washington D.C. on Jen's birthday and having a quiet supper with some of her close military friends. I thought that sounded like a nice way to honor Jen. I also wanted to speak to the military authorities. I had a lot of questions to ask.

I phoned Colonel Kessling, the Commanding Officer, USMC, and asked if he would be willing to meet with me. He agreed to and we set the date for January 12, which was a Friday. I asked Diane if she wanted to go and she agreed to join me. I booked two flights into Washington National.

A few days later, I began experiencing abdominal pain, not severe, but there was definitely something wrong. I called my doctor and made an appointment for January 11.

In addition to Jen's forthcoming birthday and my physical challenges, the training session for the leadership program was scheduled in Detroit for January 9 and 10.

I attended the first day of the training. There were approximately six to eight trainers in the group. I was barely "Scotch-taped" together emotionally. I can only imagine the impression I must have made. At one point, one of the trainers was asking me some questions. She was trying to get to know me, as was normal for people who would be working together. I was so afraid she would ask me if I had any children. I didn't want to "lose it" the very first time I met my new colleagues. I was not very talkative and steered the conversation away from me.

At the end of the day, I left the training session very quickly. That evening I was planning to attend my first bereavement group meeting. It would take me an hour to drive home, with an additional thirty-minute to drive to the meeting. Again, I must have seemed anti-social, bolting from the center as I did.

I heard about the bereavement group from my friend, Joyce. She had a client who attended. It sounded like something I really needed to do. I didn't want to go by myself, so I asked my cousin, Jim, who had recently moved back to the Toledo area, to accompany me, which he agreed to do.

A few days prior to the meeting I spoke with Jerry and Diane, the facilitators of the group. They were so helpful and understanding, and were the first to greet me upon my arrival. I then saw Debbie, a friend from high school, who lost her daughter, Megan, in a car-train accident three years before. I didn't know she attended these meetings. We embraced and sat next to each other in chairs arranged in a circle. At the beginning of the meeting, people introduced themselves and talked about how they lost their child. I couldn't say anything. I just sat there and cried, while Debbie held my hand.

It was very helpful to hear other bereaved parents talk about their feelings. I finally felt like I found people who understood. Diane shared she her son's coat was still hanging in their closet, eight years after his death. She said there were times when she would take it out of the closet and smell it, trying to recapture the scent of her son. When I heard that, I breathed a sigh of relief. There were still thirty boxes of Jen's things in the garage, not to mention her belongings in closets and other places in the house. I felt if Jerry and Diane still had some of their son's things after eight years, there was no hurry for me to do anything after only three months. I couldn't bear to part with her things. I hadn't even gone through all of the boxes at this point. I decided I may just keep them the rest of my life. Whoever buried me would have to deal with them. I was sure it would be less painful for them.

That evening when I got home, I remembered a dream I had the night before. In the dream, I was sitting in a sewing circle with some friends from high school. We were collectively working on a quilt. It then hit me—the dream foretold of the evening to come—that I would sit in a circle with friends from high school, and mending would take place! The metaphor of sewing different pieces of cloth together was a perfect description of the journey of grief—picking up the pieces of your life, and with help, sewing them back together. I did not consciously know Debbie would be at the meeting. How did the "dream-maker" know?

On Thursday, January 11, I went to see my family physician, Dr. Elkhatib. He asked about my abdominal symptoms and what had been going on in my life. I burst into tears and told him about Jennifer. He tried to console me, saying she was now at peace. Little did we know six months from now, he and his family would be thrust into their own canyon of grief.

He ordered some tests for the next day. We both agreed I shouldn't be traveling at this point until we knew what the problem was.

I called Col. Kessling that afternoon and explained I was ill and needed to cancel my appointment. I also called Meredith and informed her I wouldn't be coming. What made me think I was emotionally strong enough at this point in time to journey to the place of my daughter's death?

The following day, on Jen's birthday, I was lying on a table having an abdominal ultrasound. As the technician moved the ultrasound wand across my abdomen, I thought about the irony of the whole situation. Twenty years ago, on January 12, I was lying on a table giving birth to my daughter. And now, I had abdominal distention and pain. Was this sympathy labor pains, or a gut in turmoil? Was my abdomen crying out for her as well? Grief was clearly being experienced at the cellular level.

Dr. Elkhatib eventually diagnosed the problem as irritable bowel syndrome, which didn't surprise me. All along, I had been describing the loss of Jen as "gut wrenching." Our bodies clearly have a direct link to our minds.

Friday, January 12, a major snowstorm hit Washington D.C., and Washington National airport was closed. I wouldn't have gotten into D.C. after all. It seemed the universe was telling me I wasn't meant to go there at that particular time. There would be another time—one I had yet to learn.

Messages in Hawaii

*All God wants of man
is a peaceful heart.*

~ Meister Eckhart

The pain of Jen's passing was not easing, and the holidays only seemed to intensify the agony and loneliness. It didn't help it was winter. The days were cold, gray, and sunless, not unlike the grief I was feeling. Needing to find some respite, I decided to spend some time in Hawaii. I've always found Hawaii to be a very healing place. I went there during other difficult times in my life, including following my separation from Tom. I knew the warm weather, gentle breezes, and sun would be good for me. I have family there and would be able to stay with them.

One day, shortly after my arrival in Hawaii in late January, I was sitting on a beach in Waikiki thinking about Jen. I was talking with her in my mind saying, *Jen, they say you're still here with me. But I can't see you; I can't feel you; I can't hear you; I can't smell you, and I can't touch you. I need a sign you are here.* My ceaseless tears were a stark contrast to the fun and frolic occurring on this beautiful beach. Even though I was sitting away from the crowds, I was becoming self-conscious about the endless rivers of water coming from my eyes and nose. I decided to walk back to my aunt and uncle's condo, where I was staying.

As I entered the door of the condo, I stopped in my tracks—the radio was playing "Vincent"—the song I associated with her death. "When all hope was lost in sight, on that Starry, Starry Night .... " I had no doubt in my mind that was a sign from her, a sign that would be validated later. I was overwhelmed.

I walked out on the lanai and was standing with my cousin Polly looking out onto the ocean. We suddenly saw whales breaching off the shore. Polly, who lived on Oahu, looked stunned as she said, "Whales never breach this close to shore. Never in all the years I've lived on the island have I ever seen anything like this!"

I, too, was in awe, but for a different reason. I remembered the time Jen and Ben adopted whales through the *Save the Whale Foundation*. Jen saved her allowance until she had enough to send to the foundation for an adoption. She received a picture of "her" whale breaching, with its tale emerging from the water. There was no doubt in my mind this was another sign from Jen. She felt a strong attachment to the whales. They were an endangered species, an evolved species—not totally understood, left to the mercy of mankind. I guess she had a lot in common with them.

That evening I had the first *visitation* dream with her. There had been an earlier dream in late October where I felt she sent me a message, but I didn't see her. In the October dream, I was going through the boxes of her belongings that were shipped to me by the military. I came across a note from her dated October 2. I started to cry. I thought it was going to be a suicide letter, but it wasn't. The note was in a telegram envelope and talked about what to do with some of her belongings. She told me that the possessions I had already given to her friends [in waking life] were exactly what she wanted me to do. She also told me where to find the Easter dress and shoes she bought for me.

In reality there were no such Easter items. I felt it was her symbolic way of telling me I had to go on. I needed to begin to rise from the dead, and believe someday, spring would come again. It was also her way of telling me the few possessions of hers I had given to her friends and family, were given exactly in accordance with what she would have told me to do. She let me know I was right on target.

On this January night in Hawaii I had the following dream:

I was in the baggage claim area at an airport. It looked more like a hangar for an airplane than an area for baggage. I was writing in my journal, recording a dream.

While I was writing, I realized that Jen walked away without saying good-bye and was leaving on a train. I left my journal and ran toward the train she was traveling on. I hopped on the side of the open-air train and shouted to her. She was standing, as one would do on a commuter train. She was current age and wearing her dress blue Marine uniform.

"Where will you be staying? I asked.

"I'll be staying with Grandma to watch the dog."

"Please call me with the phone number so I know how to reach you," I asked.

"I will."

I said to her "Maybe you could come and see my new house. I hadn't moved into it yet. (At the time of the dream, there was no new house in waking life, but there was to be one in the near future I was unaware of.)

There were a lot of people on the train. It continued to move at a fairly rapid speed. I told the conductor I had to get off. He said I'd have to jump. I did so and tumbled down a hill.

I woke up sobbing. It was so real; she was so real. I felt as if she were really there. She said she would get in touch with me and let me know where she was. She told me she would be with my (paternal) grandmother Alice, who passed over. Jen was the first and only great-grandchild Gram saw before her death. Jen also said she would be watching a dog. My grandmother did not have a dog, but my niece Lindsay's dream where she saw Jen with Sarge, the family dog, came to mind. In addition, Jen's reference to a dog in this dream would also be validated later.

She was in her dress blues, the uniform in which she was buried. There was only one place the train was heading—the other side. I knew I needed to get off. The conductor firmly told me I had to jump. As I did, I tumbled down a hill, certainly an apt description of what grief is like, although it's more like falling over a cliff.

When the realization of the dream symbolism hit me, I cried again. This was the first indication something inside me wanted to survive, knew I had to survive. I couldn't go where Jen was going—not yet. It wasn't my time.

"Starry Starry Night," the whales and the visitation dream—three more messages from her. They brought me some solace, but I wanted more.

I wanted to hear from Jen directly. I appreciated the signs she sent, but they weren't enough. I needed to hear *her* tell me she was all right, and that her death wasn't my fault. I knew I needed to see George Anderson. I had no doubt he was capable of discerning messages from those on the other side. I didn't know where or how to reach him. When I returned from Hawaii, I wrote a letter to Joel Martin, the author of *We Don't Die*, asking him how I could get in touch with George. I sent it in care of his publisher.

Toward the end of March, I received a response back from the George Anderson Grief Clinic in New York. The letter informed me of the option of a group session or private discernment at George's office in Long Island. It gave the next available dates for both, which to my dismay, weren't until December 1996, and the beginning of January 1997.

I definitely wanted a private discernment, which allowed one other person to be with me. If there were more than two people the price increased. I was a bit taken back by the cost, which was $1,000.

When my friend, Gail, and I were discussing it, she asked me, "What would you pay to hear from Jen again?"

"Anything," I replied.

"Then what's there to decide?" she said. "My only concern," she continued, "is what if Jen doesn't come through?"

"My Dad or Gram will," I replied. "They will tell me how Jen's doing. But you know what Gail? I *know* she'll come through!"

I invited Diane to come with me, which she agreed to do. I purchased a cashier's check for $1,000, circled the first available date, December 2, 1996 and mailed it. I was disappointed to have to wait so long. My only choice was to leave it in God's hands and go on with my life the best I could.

When my confirmation letter came back, my appointment was scheduled for October 21, two months sooner than the earliest date they said was available, and so close to the first-year anniversary of her death! I marveled at the synchronicity and looked forward to hearing from Jennifer.

–16–

The Most Difficult Birthday of My Life

What is to give light must endure burning.

~ Viktor Frankl

The week of February 19 was my first week as a facilitator in the leadership program. I audited the seminar the week before I left for Hawaii. Now, I was one of six facilitators leading the conference. There was a lot of pressure on me to "perform." At the beginning of the seminar, each facilitator goes in front of the group to do a piece of the conference introduction. It is also an opportunity to introduce ourselves. We have a choice to use a hand-held microphone, or wear a lavaliere. I decided to use a handheld mike. Mistake! My hand shook so badly, it was embarrassing.

Later, Harry and Colin, the two fellows in charge of the program commented on my apparent nervousness. There were 150 people in attendance. They asked if I had ever been in front of an audience that large.

"Yes," I responded.

"Then why were you so nervous?" Harry asked.

"I just don't have the reserve to draw from at this point in time."

They were both psychologists and were aware of Jen's death, but I don't think they had any idea what kind of pressure I was under. Their main concern was to provide an excellent seminar, which is as it should be.

I used every ounce of "reserve" just to survive the traumatic blow I had been dealt. It would be like a car radio running only on the battery for an extended period of time. Any drain on the battery normally is recharged by a running engine. Without the constant recharging, something like turning on the lights may cause the battery to give out.

I was still suffering from abdominal discomfort, so I wasn't in the best of shape physically. I wasn't sleeping well. I continued to awaken several times during the night, each time experiencing the "blow" of reality, and the inability to fall back to sleep.

It also took enormous energy for me to "box up" the ever-present feelings of grief and to "put on a happy face!" As if that weren't enough, my performance this week would determine if I was asked to join the team. It was a formidable challenge. I was not off to a good start.

I felt like a baseball player, who had recently been traded from the minor leagues to the majors, and just before the first game, breaks his leg. The other players are running around, performing at their best, while this player hobbles along in a cast. "What's so great about this one?" they might ask. "Why is he being considered for the team?"

Only my "cast" was invisible, one very few people interacting with me would know about. They never had the opportunity to see me in action before I was "broken." I was doing the best I could under the circumstances, but I knew how much I was not performing at 100%. How could I? It was a very humbling time.

To my relief On March 15, my birthday, I was finally told I was officially part of the team. I had been plodding along almost five months without a contract. But I drove home in tears anyway. This was my first birthday without Jen. What was there to celebrate?

My sister, Mary, was throwing a St. Patrick's Day party the next day. She asked if I would come out to her house and help prepare the food. I said yes. When I arrived, she surprised me with a small birthday dinner, with only immediate family there. They helped to ease some of the isolation and pain.

People sometimes talk about which birthday they found most difficult. Some say their 40th, some say 50th. I have a feeling my answer will always be my 45th.

Am I
Still a Mother?

Making the decision to have a child—it is momentous.
It is to decide forever to have your heart go
walking around outside your body.

~ Elizabeth Stone, Author

Easter followed a few weeks later, which was painful as well. Thoughts of decorating eggs with Jen came flooding back. My niece, Lindsay, made me a colored egg with an angel on it. It was her way of saying, "I miss her, too."

The next hurdle I had to face was my first Mother's Day without Jen. The anguish I felt as that day approached was crushing. My family was talking about taking my mother out for breakfast. In years past, we always celebrated Mother's Day in one of our homes. Why did they pick **this** year to be in a public place on a day I could hardly bear to face? Didn't anyone realize how hard this day was going to be for me?

I went to mass that morning. It never occurred to me the priest might recognize the mothers in attendance. When he asked all the mothers to stand for a blessing, I burst into tears. I sat glued to my seat. Was I still a mother? I bolted from the church as quickly as I could. I vowed I would never again attend mass on Mother's Day. I ultimately did join my family for a Mother's Day dinner at the restaurant, because after all, I still wanted to celebrate my mother. She would not have understood my absence.

That evening I wrote in my journal:

Is this what every holiday or special event is going to be like? Is life becoming for me a matter of enduring one assault after another? How long will this pain go on? It's like having someone reach into your chest and rip your heart out without anesthesia, explode a bomb in your brain, tie your guts up in knots, and throw you over the edge of the Grand Canyon in the middle of the night. For the rest of your life, you have to journey back up the canyon in the dark. You can't think clearly, everything hurts, and you can't see what's in front of you. You are tired from the climbing, and you don't see an end in sight.

I'd like to scrap this lifetime and start over. I wish I could place a phone call to God and say, "Beam me up, Scottie. I've had it with this lifetime. Let me come home, rest a while, and then we'll start over."

I feel like a POW in a concentration camp. I'm stuck here for the duration of my sentence, which I think is going to be a long one. I've always felt I would live until I was 84.

The problem is, I think if I end my life, I'll be in big trouble spiritually, karmically. It has been said there's a price to pay for ignorance. There's a bigger price to pay for knowledge. We're held accountable for what we know. So, there's nothing to do but to live out this lifetime and hope by the end of it, I've paid enough dues so the next dimension or lifetime won't be so bad.

This is truly a "dark night of the soul." I know what being a tortured soul feels like. My sleep is greatly disturbed and my gut is still a mess. There is "no joy in Mudville." Aren't I supposed to be getting better?

I feel as if I'm in the movie *Groundhog Day*—like I'm in an endless, unchanging time warp.

"One day more, this never-ending road to Calvary."[3]

Does anyone on this path ever get to acceptance? Does it ever stop hurting? What do I do with these arms that long to hold my child, and these lips that long to kiss her? How do I fill this huge hole in my heart? How do I turn off this brain that torments my sleep? Have I been so rotten this is all a payback?

I feel like a foreigner in my own country. I feel so isolated, so alone. How could I go from a family of four, to looking only at my own miserable face in the mirror—seeing these sad, defeated eyes staring back at me? How could anyone stand to be around me these days? I can't stand to be around myself.

Deliverance ... when?

I am tired of this existence. I am tired of hearing clichés from people who are well-meaning, but who couldn't possibly understand this type of grief. I know they are only trying to help, but sometimes what they say makes it even worse. Things like:

"God never gives us more than we can handle." So, does that mean if I had been a weaker person, I might still have my daughter? That doesn't make me want to continue to be strong. Let's see what else He can throw my way. Maybe if I just totally fall apart, He'll see I can't handle anymore. Besides, He evidently gave Jen more than she could handle. Perhaps it is better said, "God will give you the strength to handle whatever you are asked to deal with."

"It was God's will." NO, I don't think it was God's will Jennifer shoot herself. God never wanted her to do that. God never wants His children to take their own lives. He doesn't want them to suffer. How could anyone know what is God's will for someone other than themselves? And even if it wasn't His will, how could He let this happen? Is it because He gave us free will?

"Only the good die young." So, what does that make all the rest of us who are still around?

This one may sound soft and gentle, but it's simply another platitude: "God wanted another flower for His garden." So, why didn't He pick an orphan who didn't have parents left to mourn, or a child whose parents are abusing him or her, or a child dying of starvation? All children are beautiful; why would He pick mine? I don't really think God goes around choosing one child over another.

And when there's nothing left to say, this one emerges: "She is better off; she's no longer in pain." Maybe so, BUT I'M IN PAIN!

Then there are those who are trying to be empathetic: "I don't think I could live if I lost one of my children!" That's exactly what I feel, but that statement makes me feel as if I shouldn't still be here. The fact I survived it thus far, that I'm still standing here, well, maybe the person was insinuating that I didn't or don't love my child as much as they love theirs.

Here's the one we probably hear the most often from people who have never walked in our shoes. "You should be over this by now;" or "Aren't you over this by now?" A parent never gets over the loss of a child. How could we? We live the rest of our lives with this incredible hole in our hearts. We take that pain to our own graves.

This has been a tough day, a tough month, a tough seven months, a tough lifetime.

I closed my journal.

It's hard to know what to say to someone who has lost a child. It's more important to listen to a bereaved parent than to speak, or to simply sit together in silence, or to hold her hand while she weeps. What helped me most is when people hugged me and told me they loved me. Fortunately, most of my family and friends knew what to say and do. They reinforced I was a good mother and that Jennifer knew I loved her. It's when I ventured into the outside world, I began to hear things that weren't so helpful. It was difficult sometimes to leave the protection of my friends and family.

–18–

He Dies with Honor, Who Cannot Live with Honor

*Always the bulk of hurt resides with the
person who's the most perceptive.
People who are not spiritually developed don't hurt
as easily nor as deeply as those who are,
because of the difference in their perception.*

~ Sylvia Browne, *Soul's Perfection*

I continued to question the military's responsibility in this tragedy. It seemed to me there were individuals who were culpable: the officer who was harassing her, the superiors who knew about her previous suicide attempt and assigned her to a post where she needed to carry a weapon, and the officers who did nothing when Jen called HMC and conveyed the message to Dick that should have alerted them to her impending suicide.

Her father and I discussed at length whether to pursue legal action against the military. I am not one who readily endorses lawsuits. I also did not want to make a decision solely out of anger or grief. However, in this case, her father and I did not want to see another young person go through what Jennifer experienced.

I talked with an attorney in Washington D.C. with expertise in military affairs. He advised we certainly had grounds for a *Wrongful Death Suit.* He also explained I could not sue individuals employed by the military. I would, in fact, have to sue the U.S. Government.

I went through incredible anguish in an attempt to make a decision on this issue. I realized if I did go forward with the lawsuit, it would be a long process. It would probably cost more money than I could afford. It would interfere with my ability to make a living—with potential trips to Washington, court hearings, and all the preparation involved. It may also interfere with the natural course of the grief process. More than likely, I would be stuck in the anger phase of grief, and my healing could be delayed for years. Also staring me in the face was the stark reality guilty people sometimes get "off the hook" simply because they have a lot of money, have a good lawyer or because of some technicality. Justice isn't always served. What chance would I have fighting the U.S. Government? Sure, the trial might impact the careers of a few individuals in the Marines, but the government is bigger than I am, and it has much deeper pockets.

In addition, I thought extensively of the other side of the coin: what if I utilized the same amount of energy, time, and resources and channeled them into a positive movement? Wouldn't the good far outweigh the token punitive measures potentially doled out to a few culpable military personnel?

As a facilitator for a leadership program, I have an audience composed primarily of men who are in leadership or management positions. They are also fathers, husbands, and community leaders. In the seminar, we talk about abuse of power, which, in my estimate, is what happened with Jennifer. The three types of abuse seemed to be exemplified by each of the key players in her demise: *overt* power abuse personified by Sgt. Wesson, *covert* power abuse, which describes Dick, and power *avoidance*—AKA Sgt. Sweeney. I experienced the consequences of abuse of power and was even more determined to help others understand the responsibility and moral obligation that comes with positions of power.

What if I could spend my time helping hundreds, perhaps thousands of people, see the effects their behavior and decisions have on the people they live and work with? That to me seemed a better way to utilize my resources, and a more productive focus for my attention.

In mid-May, about the time I was trying to finalize my decision regarding a potential lawsuit, a major story hit the news. I just finished a meeting and decided to stop on the way home and get some lunch. I walked past a news stand and halted when I saw the headlines: "Navy's Highest-Ranking Officer Commits Suicide!" Admiral Jeremy Boorda, a four-star admiral, had taken his life when his honor was questioned.

My God, Jennifer, I thought, with all due respect to Adm. Boorda, *You are in prestigious company. If a man of his stature and credentials takes his life because his honor is threatened, then what was a young, inexperienced Lance Corporal to do? What is this pride thing with the Navy and Marines anyway? Is it like the ancient Japanese culture?* Scenes of the opera, *Madame Butterfly*, flooded my memory: "He dies with honor, who cannot live with honor." Even if one did nothing dishonorable?

My heart went out to Admiral Boorda's family and associates. What a tragic way to end a career for which he had every reason to be proud! His death affected me greatly. I began to think, "What if pursuit of legal actions did end the career of someone in the military? What if they, in turn, took their own lives? Could I live with that?"

In the days and weeks that ensued, after considerable deliberation, I reached a decision—*God would be the final judge.* Each of the individuals involved would someday come face to face with God and with themselves. They would see everything they did, or didn't do, that may have contributed to Jennifer's demise. They would have to feel her pain and mine. In the meantime, they had to live with themselves. They would have to look at their reflection in the mirror every day as well as to gaze upon their own daughters, or daughters-to-be, and always live with the question, "Could I have done things differently with LCpl Merrihew?" I was certainly asking myself that question every minute of every day.

–19–

One Day More

The depth of my grief
is a constant with the breadth of my love.
I would never sacrifice one
to avoid the pain of the other.

~ Molly Fumia, *Safe Passage*

I needed to finalize the necessary arrangements for my trip to New York to see George Anderson. I had enough frequent flyer miles to book flights for both Diane and me. Even though reserving frequent flyer seats for a specific day can often be a challenge, I had no trouble getting two seats for a weekend flight into LaGuardia.

I thought it might be nice to treat Diane to a Broadway play for her birthday, which was October 18, three days before the reading. Without any difficulty, I was able to get two second-row seats for *Les Misérables*, which was currently playing at the Imperial Theater on 46th and Broadway. I was amazed.

I had enough Marriott points to get a free night at the Marriott on Broadway, if they had an opening for October 20. They did! What's more, I had a coupon from one of the rental car companies for two free days of rental, which I was also able to arrange. I was amazed everything worked out so easily. I felt even more encouraged that going to see Anderson was indeed what I was supposed to do. As I always do before beginning any endeavor, I said my usual prayer, "Not my will, but Thine be done. If this is not right for me, then shut the doors." All doors were wide open, and all systems were "go."

I told very few people I was going to see George. I didn't want to hear anyone's opinion about mediums, or whether they felt I should be doing this. I was never so sure about anything in my life. I knew I had to see George if I was ever going to survive this. I was being destroyed by profound guilt and grief. It didn't matter how many people told me Jen's death wasn't my fault and that I was a good mother. I had to hear it from Jen. I knew she was not in Hell, but I also needed to hear she was doing all right "over there." If I knew she was okay, I could go on. It wouldn't take away the grief, but maybe it would help to decrease the guilt and anxiety.

I gradually began to tell people about the book, *We Don't Die*, to prepare the way in the event I did want to share my Anderson experience with them. If they read the book and seemed open and interested in the subject matter, I brought them into my confidence. If they showed no interest in the book, or reacted in a fearful or judgmental way, I didn't discuss it any further.

I talked out loud to Jen about the visit with George. I told her, "Jen, I know I am the first person in my family to do something like this. I have a lot of relatives over there and there's probably going to be a crowd. You just push your way through the crowd. You don't even have to be polite."

Then I realized what I was saying and decided I'd better have a few words with my father and grandmother as well. I said, "Dad and Gram, I love you and I want to hear from you, also. But I need to hear from Jen. Please do everything you can to help her communicate. Give her as much time as she and I need." Later, at the reading, I would be astounded to see they not only heard me but respected my wishes!

The first anniversary of her death was approaching. As each day brought me closer to that fateful day, it was like reliving it all over again:

my sister and brother-in-law's first wedding anniversary—a reminder of the last time I ever saw her; the change of seasons to fall—signaling the moment my life had changed forever.

I blocked out October 2 on my calendar. I would not be working that day. I planned to go to mass and visit Jen's grave. I requested masses for Jen be said at my church on the second of every month. I attended as many of them as I could. As Catholics, we are taught to pray for the dead. But what influenced my decision to pray even more than my Catholic heritage were the readings by Anderson in the Joel Martin books. I read repeated examples where spirits thanked those who prayed for them, and consistently mentioned prayer helps them to advance on the other side.

I also said the rosary for Jen every night. I wondered one evening, what type of prayer was more powerful: the rote prayers such as the "Our Father" or the prayers where we say the words in our hearts. I wondered if the redundant prayers did anything. She would also address this at the Anderson reading.

The time had finally arrived for the trip to New York. We flew into LaGuardia, got our rental car, and drove to the Marriott. After getting settled in our room, we dressed and went to the Imperial Theater for the matinee performance of *Les Misérables*. The show was fantastic. During the finale to act one, the entire ensemble was on stage singing a song called, "One Day More!" "One day more! Another day, another destiny. This never-ending road to Calvary ..." As their beautifully blended voices sang: "Tomorrow is the judgment day. Tomorrow we'll discover what our God in Heaven has in store ...,"[4] Diane and I looked at each other wide-eyed. That indeed described our situation as well. Tomorrow we would discover what our God in Heaven had in store!

I woke up the next morning remembering the following dream:

I walked into a clinic. There was something wrong with my eyes, and I needed to get a procedure done for some time. Diane was with me. She stayed in the waiting room while I went up to the nurse's desk. It was the end of the day. I told the nurses who I was. There were four nurses dressed in traditional white uniforms with caps. An older nurse, who had to be in her 70's, began to take large packets of salve or ointment off a shelf. She took me into a treatment room. I asked her if the doctor was in. She said, "No."

I asked her if she had his orders there. She smiled and chuckled in an impish way and said, "No."

How will she know what to do? I thought. Suddenly, I couldn't even remember what was wrong with my eyes. I just knew I hadn't been able to see as well as I would like to. She said she thought the doctor said I had a glioma, a tumor in the brain or spinal cord. I wondered if I should leave the clinic and not have the procedure done."

The dream certainly symbolized what I was about to experience. The problem was in my brain—with my thought processes and the way I was blaming myself for Jen's death. My eyes would be opened, symbolically speaking, by Anderson's reading, and I would forever see things differently.

–20–

Jennifer Busts Right Through

What would life be if we had no courage to attempt anything?

~ Vincent van Gogh, Dutch painter (1853–1890)

When we got to George's office, which was in a clinic, I went to the desk to announce to the clinic personnel, who, by the way, were dressed in white, that we were George's six p.m. appointment. We did not give our names.

Diane and I sat in the waiting room until the time of our reading, or *discernment*. While we waited, I said to Diane, "I wonder if Jen is with us, or in there with George."

When we were ushered into George's office, he quickly made sure we didn't introduce ourselves. He asked us to sit down, and he began to explain how he liked to work. He told us to just answer *yes* or *no*, unless he asked for more information. After securing permission from George to tape, I started my recorder and he began. (Note: I am the one responding to George, unless otherwise indicated.)

"We shall begin then. Keep it at *yes* or *no*. Well, a male presence has come into the room. I'm sure a male close to you has passed on somewhere. Someone is indicating a link by going like this .... " George brings his index finger and middle finger together in a scissors-like motion to show us what the spirit is doing. "Now, I'm going to assume you all are family?"

"Yes."

"Because, that's usually what the link means, family by blood, through marriage or choice. The link comes again (which meant a strong bond). You all are a family by blood?"

"Yes."

"There's also a female presence in the room, and another one. There are two females of two different generations, because one seems older, one seems younger; other people are flocking in, so I have a crowd here now. I'm picking out bits and pieces of their conversation. I don't understand, and I don't know if you will or not, but don't explain, someone in that crowd is stating 'Dad is here,' does that make sense?"

"Yes."

"Don't explain, but I'm also overhearing somebody talking about a daughter who has passed on. Does that make sense?"

"Yes."

"See, this is why it is easy for me to tell you and then ask. Because it may mean something else other than what I would think. There's also talk of Mom."

"Yes."

"I hear it all in the background. So, there must be people ... either they are these people, or they're talking about these people. And this is where I'm lost for the moment. Yeah, again someone is bringing up the loss of daughter; does that make sense?"

"Yes."

"Well, I'm going to have to question. You lost a daughter?" He looks directly at me.

"Yes."

"Okay, because that's what I'm assuming; they're bringing it up and they're not saying anything. I'm like, 'Did this lady lose a daughter? Did this one? Did somebody over there?' And they just said, 'Well, ask!' Because, I've established it already. But her daughter is related to you (He looks at Diane)—yes? Yeah, because she says you're a family, of course. So, your daughter is present. Oh yeah, that could be why I'm hearing, 'Mom is here; Mom is here' ... in front of me. Her dad is still living, too, yes?"

"Yes."

"Wait a minute, there is talk of loss of a father. Did that make sense?"

"Yes."

"Did your dad pass?"

"Yes."

"Okay, because your daughter brings it up again. She starts talking about the loss of a father, grandfather, so in this case it is your father. And there's also talk of loss of a father-in-law, so is it yours as well?"

"Yes."

"So, must be that her two granddads are with her, because somebody refers to your 'husband's father' and said that Dad is here again. So apparently your daughter is there with her two granddads."

(To Diane) "Am I safe in assuming this is your niece?"

"Yes," Diane replies.

"Okay, because she keeps coming to you as a mother essence. It's obvious you're not her grandmother, so this has to be your niece then, because the other mother essence would be an aunt. You and she were very close, because it's like you lost a daughter, too. She recognizes she comes to you as your niece, but in an emotional way you are like her second mother and she states you feel like you've lost a daughter also. You certainly can sympathize what your sister, her mom, is going through. Now, she is speaking of a young male. Can I assume she has a brother?"

"Yes."

"One she was very close with?"

"Yes."

"Because apparently, she is calling out to a brother, speaking about a male, a brother, one that she is obviously very close to, that they were good friends, as well as brother and sister. Now your daughter singularizes herself, which can have different meanings. I'll give you the meanings and we can pick one or two. It can mean she's the only daughter, the eldest or youngest."

"She's the only child; this is a stepbrother."

"Oh, okay. So, in this case that's another reason it hits home so bad; she's not only the only child, but also the only daughter, in this case of obviously calling to her brother. Because it may be stepbrother, stepsister, but they still were close."

"That's right."

"Closeness as brother and sister, good pals, plus there's the feeling of him really not knowing how's he's supposed to feel in this."

"Yes."

" ... because again, it's bad enough being bereaved parents, but a sibling almost doesn't feel they have an identity, which of course they do, and that's why in a lot of ways her brother suffers in silence."

"Yes."

"Your daughter speaks of passing tragically. Is that correct?"

"Yes."

"She says she passes tragically. She states it is beyond her control; that's correct?"

"Apparently."

"That's what she states. I'm going to have to go with what she says. She states it's beyond her control. She also apologizes for the passing. You understand?"

"Yes."

"It becomes beyond her control, yes?"

"Could be ... "

"That's what she states. I don't know what she means; I'm just repeating back. But she does apologize for the passing. Her dad is still on the earth, yes?"

"Yes."

"Does she have a father and a stepfather?"

"Yes."

"Yes, because she's calling out to both."

"Is she?"

" … her biological and her step-dad. Did she and her natural father have a little lack of communication?"

"Yes."

"But she does call to both her fathers with love. Because she admits, she and her natural father have a lack of communication. She's like 'oh, so what else is new?' and there wasn't really a chance to tighten that gap, but she says she doesn't hold anything against him over there; she just wants to bring that up. But she was close with her step-dad?"

"No."

"Because she draws close to him, but maybe that's why. Maybe if there was a lack of communication, she calls to him. Your daughter admits she could give him a run for his money."

"Yes."

"She says, 'It takes two to tango.' She says, 'I forgive and hope he does, too.' Because he has been affected by her passing, in his own way. Probably this is why she's drawing close to him from the hereafter, because there was a lack of communication. And as she states, 'I forgive and hope he does too.' She says, 'He could get off some bulls-eyes,' but so could she. She might have thought at times he was a S.O.B."

"Yes."

" … but she was a bitch." (Laughter) "She says, 'I might have thought he was a son-of-a-bitch, and he might have thought I was a bitch.' But it's funny, deep down inside they liked each other."

"Is that right?"

"It's almost like a love-hate relationship. She also apologizes that at times you might have felt in the middle."

"Yes."

" … because she definitely busted your chops as well."

"Yep!"

"She says, 'I'm sorry I made you feel you weren't a good enough mother (I break down at this point), where you might have felt you were always doing things wrong all the time, where you were screwing up your life and everybody else's, when you were trying your best to put everything together.' She just wants you to know she always loved you and still does, even though she had a very bizarre way of showing it. Because, your daughter admits that, as much as she gave her stepfather a run for his money, she certainly gave you a run for your money also."

"Yes, she did."

"She also admits, and this is no reflection on anyone else, she wasn't the happiest person here on the earth."

"That's correct."

"She just didn't like it here, and I think we all have days like that, some more than others; she says, 'It's no reflection on my mother, my stepbrother, my father ... nobody. I just didn't like it there.' Because in a unique way she was kind of a spiritual individual ... "

"Yes."

" ... that she was probably more suited, *is* more suited for the next dimension. I keep hearing that song they sing about that painter Vincent Van Gogh."

"Oh, I knew that was coming!" Diane exclaimed with her eyes as big as saucers. We both burst into tears.

–21–

Peace Be with You

Jesus himself stood among them and said to them,
"Peace be with you."

~ Luke 24:36, *The Holy Bible*

George allowed us to collect ourselves and continued, "Apparently that song has meaning for you."

"Yes."

"She knows it does, and that's why she's stating it accordingly. Because in her essence as the song states, she is a beautiful person … "

"Yes."

" … but she's just not suited for this existence."

"Yes."

"Your daughter is happy to be able to tell you through me hearing that song sung from the hereafter, not only is this a unique clue that you're hearing from her, but also this is how you know she's happy in the hereafter; and she knows that's all you have to know; you just have to know she's happy over there and she's all right. Yeah, you prefer to have her here, I'm sure; but since you know that cannot be, if she must be there, as long as she is happy and at peace, that's all you care about. And she wants to let you know that you can go home and have a good night's rest because she has found herself in the hereafter. Yes, she could have done it on the earth, but she really didn't give herself a chance. I don't want to sound overwhelming by saying it's her fault, but she admits it was her fault, that she really didn't give herself a chance to find herself in this dimension.

"She seems to be prone to a great deal of moodiness here, because she claims she's inclined to be very temperamental. She admits that if she had a bug up her rear-end about something, you knew about it."

"Yes."

"And actually, she knows you were eager for this session, but you were kind of anxious, because you were almost afraid she might get a little hostile."

That puzzled me because I wasn't afraid of that.

George continues, "But she says, no, it simply isn't the case. If she has an ax to grind with you, you'll hear about it, but 'There's also a responsible way of doing it,' as she states. Actually, interesting, your daughter was very creative, yes?"

"Yes."

"Again, I hear that song, but I see paintings, so I'll take that as a symbol of creativity, that she was very creative, that she was, and is, a very sensitive individual. But unfortunately, here on the earth, sometimes her sensitivity would be her downfall, because it put her on the defensive. She took things to heart too much.

"She admits ... there's a tremendous showing (of people) at her wake and funeral ... "

"Yes."

" ... because she thought nobody liked her. And she felt that ... she admits she was inclined, I'm not saying she's a mental case, but she admits she was inclined to be a little paranoid, thinking people didn't like her, that they were talking about her, that she wasn't good enough. She was terribly hard on herself, and it was due to her own sensitivity. And she states, seeing so many people showing up at her wake and funeral kind of turned her around a great deal, that people did sincerely like her.

"She thanks you for the memorial, where she states good things are being done in her name." (Memorial donations were made to the Make-A-Wish foundation. A young child with a brain tumor got a computer with the money donated in Jen's name.)

"Her name is inscribed? She talks about her picture and her name inscribed. I don't know what she means so I hope you understand what she's talking about."

"Yes." (She was talking about her tombstone, which has her military picture "diamond-etched" on the front and her senior high school picture on the back.)

"Also, I see the rosary; someone is saying the rosary for her?"

"Yes."

"I keep seeing white rosary beads in the room, and I see our Lady of Lourdes appearing, and your daughter thanks you for saying it for her. Your daughter's not a religious person, but she was spiritual in her own way. And she just doesn't want you to think you're wasting your time. Sometimes you might feel you're being redundant, and it's not doing anything, but it is. As she says, 'You'll pray with more fervor now because you'll know you're not wasting your time.'"

I recalled my question regarding rote prayers and if they really helped. Jen provided the answer.

"She just wants you to know she's not mad at you. I don't know if that thought crossed your mind. She keeps telling me she wants you to know she's not mad at you; she certainly loves you and knows you're a good mother, and you have not failed her as a mother. You've tried so hard to do everything right in your life, and it always seems to you like you have been screwing up someplace. She says you've got to start to give your mind and heart a break now, realizing you're doing your best, and if your best isn't good enough for everybody else, well that's not your fault. You're still honestly doing your best, and that's what you should recognize."

There's a long pause as George struggles with what he's hearing. He then says, "I don't know how I'm going to explain this, because I don't want to give the wrong impression, but your daughter admits she wanted to pass on; does that make sense?"

"Yes." As I was in the midst of severe emotional pain and profound grief, I could relate to a person's desire to pass on.

"She says she didn't want to be here, that she wanted to pass on. So apparently when the opportunity came, she was ready to let go."

At this point George listens and seems to struggle with what he's hearing. He talks with Jennifer for a moment and then says to me, "Your daughter states she did not commit suicide; does that make sense? Yes, she takes her own life, but she doesn't commit suicide. That's why I was making faces. I'm like ... 'How do I explain this?' Because I just saw Jesus appear behind you and say, 'Peace be with you and peace be with your daughter also.' Yes, she takes her own life, but she doesn't commit suicide. Maybe she'll explain what she means. But she wants you to know she's not suffering in Hell."

A wave of relief hits me. I was so worried about her suffering as a result of her actions. Once again, Jen addressed an issue causing great anxiety for me.

"Because, that's been a big hang-up. You must have been raised Catholic!"

"Yes, of course!" I say as Diane and I laugh.

"But again, even though in your heart you don't want to believe that, there's still that indoctrination from your Catholic upbringing that could have happened. Interesting, because again Jesus appears behind you saying, 'Peace be with you, and peace be with your daughter also.' So that should answer it. As your daughter states, 'If you're capable of mercy and compassion, what makes you think they're not over there?' Probably even greater; I would expect more of it from over there.

"She passes in a sleep? Because she tells me she goes over in a sleep. The actual transition might have been the case."

I was so relieved to hear she did not have to view the scene she left in the physical body, as is often described by those who have survived a near-death experience.

"Now she's speaking about a weapon. Is there a weapon involved?"

"Yes."

"Because there is a weapon involved, but the thing is ... I think I can safely say your daughter is not in the right frame of mind when this occurs. She kills herself, but doesn't commit suicide. Um, to be honest with you, I almost feel as if she had a little bit of a nervous breakdown,"

"Yes."

" ... and didn't know it. Because I see screws ... she's obviously screwed up in the head. I don't mean that offensively. I'm trying to say it as directly as possible. Uh... this could be a symbol ... I'm hearing gunshot ...."

"Yes."

"There is a gun involved. Because she said there is a weapon involved and that could be symbolic, and then I heard a gunshot go off. Yeah, it makes her go to sleep ... her spiritual self goes to sleep. Shot to the head?"

"Yes."

"Yes, she's talking about shooting to the head, shot to the head. Was the weapon loaded funny?"

"I don't know."

"It's funny ... I keep hearing that song out of the musical *Annie Get Your Gun*, 'I Didn't Know the Gun Was Loaded.'"

"Oh, my God!" Diane exclaims.

Twice I played the role of Annie Oakley in *Annie Get Your Gun*! Jen came to rehearsals with me and knew all my lines and songs, including the song, "You Can't Get a Man with a Gun." I performed in dozens of plays, but Jen picked the one that was mentioned in her eulogy.

"Does that make sense?" George asked.

"*Annie Get Your Gun* certainly makes sense," I responded.

"Oh, then I've interpreted my message wrong, and I just got yelled at, that I should have stated what I saw first, and then asked you if the gun was loaded funny. Because, I first heard the song 'I Didn't Know the Gun Was Loaded' ("You Can't Get a Man With a Gun") from *Annie Get Your Gun*, and I interpreted it, and then as soon as I did, and you didn't seem to understand what I meant when I said 'Was the gun loaded funny,' somebody yelled at me and said, 'Why don't you say what

Joyce Harvey in her role as Annie Oakley singing
"You Can't Get a Man with a Gun"

you saw and then question?' So, apparently my interpretation is wrong, but what I saw has meaning. So, you understand what she's driving at; she's obviously trying to give you clues to let you know most emphatically you're hearing from her; also, so this can put your mind at ease. It will not put your mind at peace once and for all, but it will certainly put your mind at peace to a degree.

"Your daughter talks of medication. Was she on it?"

"Yes."

"Because she's bringing up she's unbalanced, and she might have been, in a lot of ways, unhinged. Plus, we're dealing with somebody who's very emotional, high-strung, and sensitive. She takes everything to heart. She just doesn't want you to feel like you were being punished by this act. You might have felt this was her final statement on you, her final testament on you, if you'll excuse my way of putting it, and this simply is not the case."

He pauses to listen and says, "If there is a mistake made here, your daughter states she has 'no one to blame but myself.' As you would know and agree, here or hereafter, not anymore, but at one point, she was always her own worst enemy."

"Yes," I said, thinking *not unlike her mother!* Jen very clearly addressed my feelings of inadequacy—that her suicide was the final grade on my motherhood report card. And that somehow, if I had been a better mother, I could have prevented it.

George continued. "You have consecrated her to the Sacred Heart?"

"Yes."

"Yeah, because I keep seeing Jesus appearing again behind you in the manifestation of the Sacred Heart of Jesus. And your daughter asks you to continue to pray to the Sacred Heart of Jesus also on her behalf, that you embrace her with that."

Upon hearing "embrace her" with prayers, I thought of my "group hug" request to Jesus for Jen every night! Plus, we had consecrated her to the *Sacred Heart*, which means masses would be said for her.

"But again," George continued, "this is not a selfish slap-in-the-face suicide. You might have thought that, but it's not true. Yes, she takes her own life, but she's not in the right frame of mind. Remember, as your daughter states, she was going through terrible depression."

"Yes."

"Depression is an illness. It's like if someone was dying of cancer and the doctor says you have six months to live, and they can't stand the pain anymore and they speed up the process. Depression is an illness also.

"She had had it up to here with people, yes?" George says as he points to his neck. "Yes, can you blame her? I can't say I disagree with her. But she said she had had it up to here with people. When she passes over, she's welcomed by animals. That's par for the course, whether they be family pets, or animals in general ... where she's taken to the 'hospital of reflection,' where she's surrounded only by animals. This gives her the chance to come out of herself, to feel at peace with herself, to start nurturing again, and to find herself. Because, the animals do not ... she doesn't have to worry about the animals making judgment on what's she's done. She's accepted and loved for the person she is. Plus, she admits, even on the earth she kind of preferred the company of animals over people anyway. Definitely can't say I blame her. We would have gotten along fine. But, yes, she admits on the earth she is not a people person."

He says directly to Jen, "Don't worry, Honey, there's nothing wrong with you. You're fine, you're normal as far as I'm concerned!" Facing us he continued, "But she certainly could be herself and could accept the love and affection of animals and exchange it. Where with people, there was always the fear, the paranoia that it wasn't sincere. She had failure in a relationship?"

"Yes."

"Yes, she's bringing up something about feeling at the time that was the straw that broke the camel's back, that the feeling of a rejection, a failure in a love relationship screwed her up."

"Yes."

"Your daughter admits, and again, she's starting from being in this *hospital of reflection*, seeing herself as she really was and is, she admits she made life an opera where everything had to be a dramatic move or gesture."

I make a big gesture with my arms, stretching them as far as I could.

"Exactly!" George says. "I keep seeing operas I go to see at the Met, and everything is very dramatic and flowery. 'Oh, it's the end' and all this, and she admits she was her own worst enemy. She made everything an opera, a drama. So again, when she felt rejected in this relationship, 'Oh there has to be a dramatic outcome to it.' Interestingly, did she ever have any aspirations for the theater?"

"Yes." (Jen was also active in school plays and community theater.)

"Yeah, because she would have made a good actress."

"Yes, she would have."

"Because she admits if she had the voice, she would have made a good opera singer because she could have acted out the tragedies of life and sung them out."

"Yes."

"I keep seeing Maria Callas appear, so she could have been like her, a good opera singer as well as an actress."

"She had a beautiful voice," I added.

"But again, here on the earth she was an artist; she was surrounded by that which was creative and artistic. And of course, those people can be eccentric, and they can be sensitive and they can be dramatic. And they can have a lot of struggles the normal person may not. And your daughter certainly falls into this category."

So does her Mother, I thought.

"She had an exchange of words?"

"Yes."

" … with you or your husband, or something? Because just prior to it happening, she speaks of an exchange of words. Now that could have been a few days, a week prior; I don't know. But she just wants to apologize. She just doesn't want you to go home thinking she is mad at you.

"She says, 'I'm not mad at you.' She says, 'Who doesn't say the worst thing at the wrong time in anger?' I do, you do. We're human.' Plus, she recognizes for the first time that you were at your wits end. You just didn't know what to do with her anymore. I get a feeling I'm stretching a violin to the limit, where the strings are about to burst. It's like 'I'm giving up on her because I don't know what to do anymore.'"

He was describing exactly what I was feeling when I wrote Jen the letter that has since haunted me.

"And, you've played referee for so long; it's like you're between her and your husband; you're trying to work things out, and you just feel you're failing. Did she leave a note or something?"

"I wrote a letter."

"Okay, cause she's talking about the letter and she says 'Let's forget about it!'"

I start crying.

"Yeah, she says, 'I forgive and I hope you do too. Let's drop it; let's forget about it.' Because, you've thought it over and you feel you've put an additional bullet into the cartridge."

"Yes." I'm sobbing at this point.

"She says, 'Stop tormenting yourself. You're worried about *me* being in Hell, you're putting *yourself* through hell.' She says you have to let go of this and just recognize that this is not the case.

"As I said, one thing about your daughter, if she had an ax to grind with you, here or hereafter, you'd hear about it.

"She admits this wasn't the right thing to do; this wasn't the right action to take. However, she admits she was not in the right frame of mind when this occurred. 'Go home and have a good night's rest,' she says, because you don't sleep well, with it constantly on your mind. Plus, you're dreaming about it and there's anxiety, and she says 'You can let it go now. You have to heal yourself.' Losing a child by death is one thing; losing a child by taking their own life makes it ten times worse, because there's so much guilt and anxiety left behind. She says this can be cleared away. 'Exorcise the demons that are haunting you. And only you can do that.'

"Again, with Jesus appearing a fourth time now stating 'Peace be with you and peace be with your daughter also.' Those words you're hearing Christ utter certainly spell it all out. So, you just have to remember to reflect on that.

"Your daughter realizes now she could have worked out a lot of her problems and indifferences on the earth. But again, she made everything an opera, plus she did have her emotional and mental state against her. Again, her depressions were almost genetic; they can be hereditary and they can be very difficult to deal with. Again, depression is still an illness, and it's only now the psychiatric and medical community is starting to recognize that. Depression is an illness that isn't so easy to mend like a broken leg.

"But your daughter wants you to recognize you did do everything possible to help her. You did, and she doesn't want you to think you didn't do your best. You're human, too. You can reach your wit's end also."

To Diane he says, "She used to talk to you a great deal?"

"Yes," Diane replies.

"Yeah, because she thanks you for always being a good sounding board, that you were kind of ... I see Switzerland ... obviously you were a neutral source of reconciliation."

Both of us laugh and agree.

"I almost started to interpret, and your niece said to me, 'Say what you see first and then explain.' This is true. As soon as I start going back to the old way [of discerning] it seems to make the reading not as powerful. But the thing is, Switzerland symbolizes neutrality, as you know. You tried to stay isolated and neutral, but that was good. You certainly didn't want to hurt your sister's feelings; you certainly wanted to serve as ambassadress of good will. But she thanks you, that not only have you prayed for her in the hereafter, but you've also been praying, helping her mom as well and the family to try to deal with it."

George says to me, "Do you belong to a support group?"

"Yes."

"Yes, she's glad you do because it does help you to kind of get a lot of steam out of your system. And unfortunately, sometimes you have to be around people who are in the same boat as you are. The only other thing too is, as your daughter says, 'Some people might be treating you as if you have the bug.' And she says 'Don't take it personally.' It's that people don't know how to handle the situation. Plus, losing a child, losing a child by this means, it's almost like in the back of their mind, could it be contagious? So, don't take it personally.

"I see palm trees around you. Are you traveling soon?"

"I'm supposed to go to Hawaii." I was planning another trip to Hawaii in January.

"Oh, okay. But you're encouraged to go, you know, because your daughter says, 'You almost feel irreverent if you have a life.'"

"Yes."

"You have got to go on with your life. But I see palm trees around you; she brought up a happy trip. You said you were supposed to go; she said 'You should go.' Staying home and tormenting yourself isn't going to make things any better. It's not going to make her think you love her any more or any less. She wants you to have a life and go on with your life. You want to know if she's happy going on with her life there. One thing about your daughter, when she snaps to attention and makes up her mind to do something, she has it achieved. And this is what she did. She recognized this wasn't the right thing to do. 'I should have really sought things out before I jumped to this conclusion.' Yes, she has the emotional struggles behind her, because she says to me, 'Be careful, Mom reads between the lines.'"

I laugh, because this is true.

"So, don't read between the lines. Listen to what's she's saying. She doesn't want you to go home and digest this, and then start thinking differently (that she meant something other than what she said.) But, your daughter states that … this isn't making light of what has happened, but she's saying it's 'water under the bridge.' You have to go on, just as she's going on with her life there. She's made up her mind to go on with her life, and she continues to progress ahead. There's talk of happy birthday; does that make sense?"

"Yes, Diane's."

"Is your birthday coming up? Okay. Because I just feel your daughter in front of the two of you with white roses talking about happy birthday, apparently wishing you happy birthday, that it is on the approach."

George says to Diane, "She also specifies you could use a vacation as well. So, maybe palm trees are around you, maybe not Hawaii, but you're definitely planning a happy trip."

Diane had a trip to Texas and Oklahoma City planned, which was one of the places she and Jen visited together.

George said to me, "Is there still a chance for you to go?"

"Yes."

"Were you thinking of canning it?"

"I haven't made the flight arrangements yet, so it's like … what am I waiting for? All I have to do is call the airlines."

"Yeah, go. 'You should go,' she says. 'Go and have a happy trip.' It's something you've always wanted to do, and now it's like, 'Well, I'm in mourning, I shouldn't.' Well, no, she says, you should go. Because again, you're still worried about her being all right. She knows you talk out loud to her, so you must know she's still around."

"Yeah."

"She says she is still with you and she says, 'Talk to me and know that I'm here.'"

Jen addressed my concern that my talking to her might keep her earthbound. She was letting me know that, not only was it was all right to talk with her, but she encouraged me to do so.

George continued, "Your father and father-in-law are there with your daughter, although, your daughter, ironically, is very independent."

"Yes."

"She may be there with family, but she still likes to do things 100% on her own. She seems like she has her own place there. She's like on an outpatient basis, as we understand it. She still clings to the company of animals the most. Not that she has any problems with any people; that's just her."

"Yes."

"As she says, the animals work with her, and she works with the animals in the hereafter. Did you lose pets of your own?"

"Yes."

"Yes, because she talks about the pets that have passed on being there. Now, I see a dog and a cat; there might have been one of each or she has one of each; you lost a dog, and she might have a cat over there as well, because she's saying about the animals being very specific in helping her to find herself again in the hereafter. And they don't have to do anything except love you unconditionally as they do. But again, being in this place with animals, you're in a non-threatening environment, and you can start to nurture again yourself, as well as that which is around you. But she is fiercely independent."

"Yes."

"I'll be honest with you; that doesn't seem to have changed. She likes her independence, doing things on her own. 'Yeah, my grandfathers are here' … not that she doesn't love them; that's very nice; but they respect the fact she likes her space. But that's just her, whether she was here or there, that would be the way it would be.

"There are other people in the background claiming to be your grandparents and such. There is a flock of people in the room that obviously are there. That could be why your dad was saying 'Mom is here.' It's probably like his mother ... other people there for her as well, that she has met. There is also the name Jack or John?"

"John."

"Passed on?"

"Yes."

My cousin John, with whom Jen and I performed in a lot of community theater, pops in to say hello, as well as my paternal grandmother, Alice.

"Interesting, your daughter ... without telling me ... your daughter has a common enough name. I mean I've heard it before, yes? It's not Mary or something, but I've heard it before."

"Yes."

"Because she's starting to build on it, and I just wanted to tell you what I'm hearing. You can shorten the name?"

"Yes."

He then goes through a process where he very quickly and accurately comes up with her name, *Jennifer*. And asks, "Was also known as Jenny at times?"

"Yes."

"Yeah, because she's coming in as Jennifer, Jen or Jenny. Yeah, but basically most of the time would be referred to as Jen."

"Yes."

"She keeps pushing the three letters ... "

"That's what she liked!" I said.

" ... emphasizing on *Jen*, she doesn't seem too keen on Jennifer."

"No, she wasn't."

" ... pushing more as being called Jen."

"Yes."

"It's funny; did anyone ever refer to her as *Jenna*?"

(A startled) "Yes!" Her friends from her sixth-grade trip to Camp Storer called her that. I think I'm the only person who knew that.

"They must have, because she also added an 'a' at the end of n; at times somebody might have jokingly referred to her as Jenna."

"She's giving me all the evidence to let you know she is here."

"I know she is."

"There's talk of the time of her passing. Are we approaching it?"

"Just passed it."

"She just wants to let you know she was very close to you on that day. As she states again, 'Always pray to the Sacred Heart of Jesus on her behalf, particularly on the first Friday of every month.' The first Fridays are the times of the Sacred Heart. Yes, because Jesus appears again as the Sacred Heart saying, 'Peace be with you, and peace be with Jen also.' This is to take you out of Hell ... "

"Yes," I said crying.

" ... because of the fact this so ... I see St. Jude, which symbolizes hopelessness; this is so out of your control. It's happened, one gunshot and 'I can't do anything about it now.' It's a feeling of my hands being tied. So, this again, with Christ appearing, is to take you out of Hell ... this is to send you home and get a good night's rest.

"She does apologize to her step-dad, so apparently they must have had some hairy relationship, and also to the stepbrother, too. She was close to him, but yet was giving him attitude. I feel like I'm close to him at one time, and we're friends and getting along. All of a sudden, I've got a bug up my rear end toward him. And he might not know what he did wrong."

"Yes."

"Your daughter says, 'He didn't do anything wrong. It was me. I was making a mountain out of a molehill.' Yes, she had her struggles and she had her difficulties here. We're certainly not making it sound as if her problems were nonexistent. She had genuine problems here, which were hard to deal with, like anyone her age. But she's saying her depressions were against her. Many times she spoke in anger. Many times she spoke in depression or despair, saying the wrong thing at the wrong time, or taking things the wrong way. She knows after a while you were instituting tough love. You didn't know what else to do. She said, 'So, now with this problem occurring, you think the worst.'

"Also, there's Bill or William?"

"Yes, my brother."

George delivers a message of love from my father to my brother. My father's personality clearly comes out at this point, and his description of my brother's personality is extremely accurate.

George continues, "Your father wants your brother to know he is near. Whether your brother believes this or not, your father could care less."

Diane and I chuckle.

"It's the message that's important, not the belief system. He says, 'Just tell Bill you've heard from me. I want to give him something to think about. I know he is going through a time of struggle. I want to let him know he's not struggling alone, that I am with him. That's all.' Your father says, 'He'll put his nose up to this, but fine ... let him. Because one of these days he's going to die and find out Dad's right, as usual anyway. So, what difference does it make?'

"Your father is speaking kind of confident in his message, very confident. 'When you go home, call your brother and tell him I spoke about him.' He says he definitely wants to see your brother's reaction."

George says to me, "There's talk of residence change. You might be changing residences up ahead. The reason I bring it up, is your daughter just wants to let you know it's all right. Because, if you move, you'll think you're leaving her behind.

He was right. I had said I could never move and leave her grave!

"This could be this year, next year, or it could be 1999. She just wants to let you know it's all right. Because, there's a part of you that won't let go. You are employed?"

"Yes."

"Yes, she's glad you're working, because in your case it's therapeutic. The important issue is your sanity. Now you have to work on healing yourself, and bringing some semblance of peace back into your heart again. It's up to you now. She says, 'I've spoken my peace and all is well. It's up to you to digest and absorb into yourself what has been declared tonight.' As she says, 'We don't mean to be funny over here, but with Jesus appearing to you five times saying "Peace be with you," you can't get any better than that.' Because this has caused so much confusion in you, you don't know whether you're coming or going. This way now, you should get your feet back on the ground again and start going forth. You do have a right to have a life and be happy and go on, and you will see your daughter again someday. Again, as long as you know she's all right, it's going to make it a little easier on you. This is what you have to reflect on, certainly without reading between the lines.

"One thing about your daughter, she doesn't waste any time. She gets right to the point and goes forth. Because the minute you sat down, and I was explaining to you, I could hear somebody say, 'Come on, will you just get going?' I wish all my sessions were like this. She is not a B.S. artist. She calls a spade a spade and she got right to it. But this is Jen; this is Jenna, letting you know she's all right and at peace. Continue to pray for her, as you have been."

George passes on a message from Jennifer to Diane, "She thanks you for being so supportive to her mother and family since this tragedy has occurred. 'It does pay to be Swiss,' she says, meaning in the neutral sense.

"With this, she tells me she's going to let my brain go. She got out what she had to say. She didn't waste any time.

"Your dad embraces both of you with love, just wanted to let you know he's near. Again, he wants you both to know he always loved you, even though at times he had a strange way of showing it. But he's here and sends his love. But it's obvious who you came to hear from and who had the need.

"Also, your father-in-law, your grandparents, and different other people that were here send their love. But it's obvious you're here to hear from Jen, of course. You have the most need to hear from her, and she has the most need to reach out to you. But she reaches out to both of you with love, and to her father, her stepfather and her brother as well. She's just wanting to heal the situation by letting them hear the message.

"Whether they believe it or not, who cares? It's the message that's important, not the belief system. She states too, 'One of these days you're all going to pass on, and find out that I'm right, as usual anyway.' She always felt she was right while she was here and she says, 'Sometimes, things like that never change!' But with that she signs off, and sends her love and especially for you to be at peace, that you're still her mom, she still loves you, and you're still her friend. Those things are very important to you. She says, 'Peace be with you until we meet again.' And with that she signs off and the others do too."

George took a deep breath as if he just finished a physical workout and exhaling said, "Boy, she didn't waste any time at all. She came in here like a house on fire!"

My words telling her to "Bust right through" echoed in my mind again. That, she clearly had done!

–22–

Spiritual Roses Manifested

I know not how such things can be;
I only know there came to me
A fragrance such as never clings
To aught save happy living things.

~ Edna St. Vincent Millay, "Renascence"

Diane and I walked out of the reading overwhelmed. I was experiencing a myriad of feelings: intense joy to have connected with Jen, amazement it truly happened, relief to hear directly from her she was all right, and a peacefulness with the resolution of some major issues between us. I was also grateful a man like George Anderson existed, and that I found my way to him. I actually felt exhilaration. I couldn't stop talking about it.

We went back to our hotel room and called a few family members who had known about the reading to give them some highlights.

We then played the tape. We laughed again at some of Jen's messages, and cried at others. Jen told me several times I was a good mother and her death wasn't my fault. She addressed the questions and issues I held in my heart: that it was all right to talk with her, that all prayer is powerful, that she got my "group hugs." She told me I needed to "digest and absorb" the information presented—my irritable bowel problem was certainly a problem with digestion and absorption. She talked about being with animals. I thought of Lindsay's dream where Jen was with Grandpa Robert and Sarge, the family dog. I also reflected on my dream of her on the train, where she says she's going to be with Grandma and the dog.

One of the most powerful moments of the reading for me was the mention of the letter I had written, which continued to torture me ever since. "Just let it go," Jen said. And, of course the mention of "Starry, Starry Night"—it *had* been a sign from her that day in Hawaii, a sign that would continue to come from her in the months and years ahead.

As we listened to the tape, I realized that every time the issue of suicide or my mothering skills came up, Jesus appeared and said, "Peace be with you." Five times He appeared. He and Jen both knew I needed repeated reassurance in those areas. Hearing it once would not be enough. I had taken her death very personally. George was quite accurate when he said, "You might have felt this was her final statement on you, her final testament on you." That is exactly how I felt … that I failed the most important job of my life.

Everything he said was absolutely, 100% accurate. My thoughts, the feelings in my heart, the conversations I had with Jen after she died. There was no fishing for information. He was on course from the moment he began. Jennifer's personality came through, as well as her sense of humor. But most of all, her deep love and concern for me was evident. I *knew* she would come through.

I later told my mother, as I shared the tape with her that I will never doubt myself again. When I feel this strongly about something, I will never let someone else tell me what I should or shouldn't do. I don't care who they are or whom they say they represent. People might have thought George was a hoax or the "work of the devil." But I was sure he would be a direct line to Jennifer and the balm my aching heart needed so badly.

I let too many people in my life try to tell me how to act, who to be, and what to believe. Never again!

The day after the reading, as Diane and I were waiting at the airport to return home, I called the Leadership Center to check for messages. The secretary answering the phone told me there were roses waiting for me. She told me they arrived yesterday—the day of the reading. I was dumbfounded. I didn't know anyone who would send flowers to me at work. I got off the phone and told Diane, "You're not going to believe this! Remember during the reading when Jen was offering you white roses for your birthday? Guess what arrived at work for me yesterday? Roses!"

The following day, I was at the Leadership Center to do a satellite broadcast. The flowers were waiting for me. They were the most beautiful bouquet of roses I had ever seen. Among the dozen of colorful roses were a number of white ones! I looked at the card. They were from a man who attended the leadership seminar the previous week, thanking me for a wonderful experience. We only said a few words to each other. I didn't understand why he would have sent me roses. Then it hit me—Jen needed someone to physically manifest the roses for her. I bet the man even wondered why he sent me flowers! I became even more convinced angels and spirits work through us to help them with their tasks.

The other astonishing thing that happened the same day at the Leadership Center was that two different people told me I looked wonderful, "like something good happened" to me. I thought maybe they heard about the flowers and were fishing for information, wondering if I had a special man in my life. I didn't think much about their comment at the time.

That evening, I talked on the phone with another instructor regarding a business question. Toward the end of the conversation he said, "Joyce, I have to tell you something. I realize I don't know you very well, but I have been so concerned about you. Your shoulders always looked like they were carrying the weight of the world, and even though you smiled at work, I could see the sadness in your eyes. But today when I saw you at the center, I noticed a huge transformation. Your shoulders weren't slumped anymore and that furrowed look to your forehead was gone. I don't know what happened, but I'm not worried about you anymore."

None of these people knew about the Anderson reading. They didn't even know I had been out of town. I kept that private. And yet, they could see a transformation had taken place, one that actually showed in my physical body. The session with George did help to take the weight of the world off my shoulders. Guilt and grief can be a heavy burden to carry. I would never stop missing her, but I could now begin the healing journey. I knew for certain she was still with me. That would have to sustain me until such time as we were reunited.

–23–

"Dear Jennifer ..."

*You are not judged on the heights you have risen
but the depth from which you have climbed.*

~ Frederick Douglass, *Narrative of the Life of Frederick Douglass*

I made it through the first anniversary of Jen's passing. I somehow managed to survive the first Christmas without her, the first Thanksgiving, her birthday, my birthday and the list goes on. I felt like I was treading water as fast as I could to keep up. I breathed a sigh of relief at having survived the first year, until it hit me—I had to do it all over again!

The holidays were rapidly approaching and I realized I had to face yet another Thanksgiving without her, another Christmas, another birthday. *Oh my God*, I thought, *how many times will I have to go through this?* I crashed!

In many ways, the second Christmas was as difficult, if not more difficult than the first. Almost always before Jen's death, if I worked hard enough and pulled myself up by the bootstraps, I could get through the various crises and challenges in my life. But this series of assaults seemed endless. It didn't matter how diligently I worked, how much I prayed, how many books I read, or how many positive affirmations I recited—I couldn't change the outcome and I couldn't seem to ease the pain. In December, I wrote the following in my journal:

> I'm tired of trying to smile as everyone shows me their Christmas decorations, smiling as others talk about how great it is to have all the kids and grandchildren home for Christmas. Where is the fine line between being pleased for them and wanting to scream, cry, and walk away? I'm so disgusted, so tired of all of this. How many more of these Christmas holidays will I have to endure?
>
> "Did you have a nice Christmas?" people will ask. "Was Santa good to you?" What do you say—that this is a lousy time of year, that it hurts every day of the year, but especially at this time when everything and everyone seems to be smearing your face in the muck of isolation? If there's ever a time that reminds me I live alone and have lost my only child, it's this time of year.
>
> Even Jen's spirit seems to be conspicuously absent. I suppose she has lots of people to attend to this time of year, not just her mom.
>
> I don't seem to care about anything anymore—not what's happening in the world, not what's on TV, and certainly not about the day-to-day concerns others seem to be caught up in. I can't ever imagine being happy again. Nothing can ever fill this void, this hole. And to lose your only child means losing all the grandchildren as well. I can't have any more children—not that another child can ever take the place of the child who has passed on, but I don't even have that option to look forward to. I can't imagine living into my 70's or 80's. People talk about wanting to live a long time. I can't bear that thought. Dying tomorrow would not be too soon. I imagine I would feel differently if I had other children, but what's the point now? Having to stick around here (on earth) feels like having to serve out my time in a prison or concentration camp. I know suicide isn't the answer, but I sure wish it were my natural time to go.

What would have been her twenty first birthday was also extremely difficult. I wrote to her the following letter:

Dear Jen,

I'm having a hard time tonight. This Sunday you would have turned 21. How can I describe the hole in my heart since you left? Nothing fills the void—not anything, not anyone. I don't know what to do with this pain and this anger. I've been bitchy lately. It's like I've gone from anger to general disgust ... just a chronic sense of having to live with one's lot, and not being able to do anything to change it—to bring you back.

I wish you would have called me and told me how desperate you were feeling. I would have gotten you out of the military—no matter what it took. I wish you would have given me one more chance to try to help you. You probably thought I wasn't hearing your desperation. I tried to call you several times over the weekend and you didn't return my calls. The morning of October 2, when I awoke, I thought about sending an e-mail message to everyone in my address book asking them to pray for you. But I had to drive to Detroit and didn't have time. I also thought if I did send a message, people would want to know why I sent it. I have often wondered since, if I had sent the message, and people were praying for you—would you still be alive today?

I wish I could have been there for you on that awful day. I wish you would have called. I tried to call you that morning on my way to Detroit. When I hit the speed dial, I accidentally dialed your work number at headquarters. I hung up because you wouldn't have been there that early. It was about 6:45 a.m. So, I called you in your room. I didn't know you had gone to the Pentagon that day or I would have called you there. I wished you would have called me on Sunday and told me you would be at the Pentagon Monday.

When I heard you were dead, I kept crying, "I want another chance!" But I'm not going to get that chance. I don't even get another chance to be a better mother—you were my only child.

Jen, I'm so sorry for all the times I was impatient, for all the times I didn't listen better, for the times I didn't understand, for the times I didn't appreciate the gift you were. I'm sorry for marrying Tom, and especially for moving you to Texas. Maybe if you and I would have stayed in Sylvania, you might still be alive today. I probably would have been miserable going through a divorce at that time—but I was miserable anyway. I was so homesick when we moved. You weren't the only one. And I ended up going through a divorce anyway. So, what did I gain? Nothing. I lost everything anyway, including the most important treasure I had—YOU!

I know I didn't spend enough time with you—right from the beginning. If I could do it all over again, I would do so many things differently. I would have never remarried. We did much better by ourselves. Why does God give young women hormones and an urge to couple up? We should have kids when we're 40 and finally starting to understand life.

I wanted so much to be a good mother. When you were two, I attended parent effectiveness classes. I read books. I bought more than I read—but the intention and desire were there. I tried so hard to better myself so I could be a good parent. But even with all that effort, I still made a ton of mistakes. I just didn't *get it* at times.

Remember the song we used to sing together: "I don't want to walk without you, Jenny" (and you would sing "Mommy")? Well, I don't want to walk without you. But I don't have a choice—and I'm pissed! Children are not supposed to die before their parents. But then, if I would have died first, you probably wouldn't have made it either, especially if I died when we weren't getting along. Then you might have struggled with guilt on top of your depression.

Anyway, happy birthday, darling. I know you don't need cellular phones or computers up there, but that's what I was planning to buy for your Christmas and birthday presents.

I would have loved to travel with you, to take you to Hawaii, and other places. I don't know, Jen. I don't know what this is all about. It makes no sense to me.

I miss you and I love you. Tell everyone up there I said to throw you a big party for your 21st! See if you can slip away to visit me in my dreams. You know, you haven't come in a long time. I think the last time was on October 2, other than your star presence on October 21 with George! By the way, did you put the thought in that guy's mind to send me flowers on October 21? I'll bet he's still wondering why he did that!

Keep in touch. You know I watch for all the signs.

Love,
Your mother

–24–
Families of Children United in Spirit

You may forget the one with whom you have laughed,
but never the one with whom you have wept.

~ Kahlil Gibran, *Sand and Foam*

Two days after Jen's birthday, I went to my bereavement support group meeting. I wondered for some time whether I should mention George Anderson to the other parents in the group. My instincts told me it would bring them peace to know their children are still with them in spirit. But spiritual mediums and communication with the dead can be so controversial. I didn't know what to do.

I wanted to at least share my experience with Debbie, my high school friend who lost her daughter in the car-train accident. I had given her the book *We Don't Die* for Christmas.

On this night in January, Debbie and I rode together to the bereavement group, as we often did. We talked about the book. I told her about my reading with George and shared some of the highlights. She seemed open to hearing more.

My family physician, Dr. Elkhatib, and his wife were at the meeting. They lost their son, Mark, the previous June in an auto accident. He had just turned 20. He and Jen were born the same year, and both had gone to Sylvania schools. I thought it was ironic a year ago I was in Dr. Elkhatib's office crying about losing Jen, while he was trying to comfort me. Six months later, his son was dead.

After Mark died, Dr. Elkhatib said to my friend, Gail, who worked at the hospital where he makes rounds, "I thought I understood what Joyce was going through until I lost my own son. Then I realized I had no idea how great her pain was until I began to experience it myself."

I gave Dr. Elkhatib a hug and met his wife, Regina. We sat next to each other in the familiar circle. By now I could at least introduce myself to the group and talk a little about Jennifer.

During the meeting, the facilitator asked if anyone read any helpful books lately. Debbie mentioned I had given her *We Don't Die* and she talked a little about it. Dr. Elkhatib (Mounir) and Regina mentioned they read all three books about Anderson as well. The discussion took off. It was one of the liveliest discussions we had experienced in our group. People were hungry to hear more, and several requested contact information for George. I felt badly I didn't have George's cards with me, which I picked up in New York. Mounir shared that George was going to be in Cincinnati in May. I was interested in finding out more. Regina mentioned she had the information at home, and I was welcome to stop by and get it.

The next day I did exactly that. Regina and I bonded right away. We talked for hours. When Mounir came home from the office, he joined our conversation. We shared many of our personal experiences with messages about or from our children.

He and Regina told me that a week after Mark died their nephew in Lebanon, Samer, called and told them he had a dream where Mark appeared. He said there was a light all around Mark and Mark told him, "I want you to know I arrived safely and I'm fine." A week later, Samer's sister, Lara, who lives in California, also had a dream about Mark. She said Mark appeared to her, holding what she described as a perfectly-shaped pear. Mounir explained pears were Mark's favorite fruit. In the dream, Mark gave the pear to Lara and then said "I have to go now; I have to run."

Lara asked him to stay longer. He replied, "I'm really busy. I have a new job."

She asked him, "What kind of job?"

He told her he welcomes newcomers. He said, "Sometimes when children first arrive, it can be difficult for them. So, I help them cross over." He told her a two-year-old boy would be arriving at nine o'clock and he needed to be there to meet him.

Mounir and Regina went on to tell me that two days after the discussion with their niece, Regina talked with her friend whose brother is a policeman in Florida. Regina's friend said her brother had been upset recently, because a few days prior, he had been called to a scene where a two-year-old boy had drowned in a pool and had subsequently been placed on a ventilator. On Tuesday (the day of their niece's dream) at noon (which would be 9:00 a.m. in California) the child's parents made the decision to turn off the ventilator.

I marveled at the synchronicity of those two phone calls. We all felt the boy in Florida was the one who Mark was greeting on the other side. It was as if God wanted to affirm Mark's message to their niece by offering them one additional piece of related information.

I shared with them what I learned from the George Anderson reading about Jen's job of working with animals on the other side. I eventually shared the tape of the reading with them and some of their family members. This was the beginning a long and close friendship with the Elkhatibs.

Over the next few weeks and months, we shared the visitation dreams we had with our children. We also discussed other signs we felt were from our kids. We talked about how much hope these signs brought and without them we would be in utter despair. We often discussed the spiritual aspects of losing our children and how we had been hungry for these types of discussions. We agreed conversations of this nature were lacking with most bereavement support groups. We understood facilitators were strongly urged not to discuss anything religious and controversial because of the varying backgrounds of the people in the group.

The Elkhatibs are Muslim and I am Catholic. Not once did we have difficulty discussing the spiritual aspects. They mentioned the Koran, and I talked about Jesus, but we never had any problems understanding each another. We seemed to be saying the same things, even though we may have used different language or symbols. The spiritual dilemmas of bereaved parents seem to be universal. Regina told me the Koran says that any mother who has lost a child goes directly to Heaven. That made sense since we've already spent time in Hell.

I said to Mounir and Regina at one point, "Even if a person never had a spiritual thought or question *before* the death of her child, she does afterward. I don't know how to process this trauma without discussing the spiritual aspects. It would be like trying to describe the sinking of a ship without mentioning the water."

We needed to make sense out of what happened to us, and where we would go from here. Living a life without our children's physical presence was devastating. However, understanding and believing their spirits were still with us took some of the sting out of the bite.

We decided we wanted to start a support group where the spiritual aspects of death, as well as life after death, could be discussed in a non-denominational way. We also wanted the group to be open to all family members including grandparents and siblings. There wasn't a group like that available in our area at this point.

We began to work out the various aspects of putting such a group together. Regina came up with the name F.O.C.U.S.—Families of Children United in Spirit. It was a perfect description of our vision for the group. We wanted to create an environment where parents could talk, not only about their grief, but also about the signs they received from their children.

In the introduction to his book, *Reunions*, Raymond Moody writes, " ... as many as 75 percent of parents who lose a child to death will have some kind of apparition of that child within one year of the loss." We soon found our children's signs weren't unique. What was unique, however, was our willingness to share this information with others.

On March 27, 1997 we held our first meeting at a local hospital. Soon our group became a place where families could say what had really been in their hearts, without anyone looking at them like they were crazy. Nobody told them how they should feel. People could shake their fist at God if necessary, and ask all the "whys" until the whys were exhausted. In this environment we could heal together.

I was worried initially about what people would say if we were talking openly about signs from, or communication with our children on the other side. But that worry paled in comparison to the gratification of seeing parents, who initially walked into our meeting with slumped shoulders and that dull, painful look in their eyes, walk out after the meeting standing taller and having a look of hope on their faces. Sometimes it was a look of relief in finding people who did not think they were crazy because they felt they had a sign from their child.

The Elkhatibs and I continued to attend both support groups for quite a while. We will always be grateful for the first group and for the bereaved parents who helped us when we could hardly put one foot in front of the other.

-25-

Premonitory Dreams

*A dream that is not understood
is like a letter not opened.*

~*The Talmud*

I was lonesome to hear from Jennifer again so I scheduled an appointment with a local medium. She was also very accurate. At one point during the reading she said, "There are a number of children here [in spirit]. They are giving you flowers, thanking you for helping their parents. Do you sit in a circle and help grieving parents?"

"Yes," I replied.

"They are so grateful to you. They are saying to you, 'If you only knew who you are.'"

"But," she continued, "you will find that out when you cross over. Only, you won't be crossing over for a long time—not until you are 84!"

Whoa! There was my confirmation of what I've felt all my life. It is unusual for a medium to expose the subject's age or method of death, but she continued her reading in a rather surprised voice. "Oh! You gave

Spirit ultimatum. When they [Spirit] told you that you might lose a child in this lifetime, you didn't want to come back. But they wanted you to come back so they agreed to your request that you die of a heart attack in your sleep!"

At that point, I about fell off the chair. It sure explained why, in my pain, I was yelling at God that He owed me a heart attack in my sleep (as if God owes us anything!). I walked out of the reading with a lot to absorb.

Regina and I had become close friends, and I introduced her to other mothers who had lost children. I had been meeting with these bereaved mothers, who were further down the road with their grief. I gained immense support from talking with them and looked forward to the monthly gatherings.

Over time, I shared with them the dreams where Jen visited, which they found fascinating. They said they had trouble remembering their dreams. I told them I had been working with dreams for about eight years, and reassured them if they began to record and work with their dreams, they would soon begin to remember them more easily. I shared with them I felt dream work helped immensely with inner growth and also with healing. They were very interested in starting a dream group, and we began to put the plans in place.

I contacted my cousin, Jim, who is a Jungian psychotherapist and skilled with dream work. He agreed to facilitate the group. It was a unique group, in that all but one member had lost a child. The group began to see the power in working with their dreams. They were gaining tremendous insights into their lives. In addition, the dreams were clearly pointing out various stages of healing with respect to the loss of loved ones.

As I looked back over dreams I had in the years preceding Jen's death, I could see how they may have been preparing me for, perhaps even warning me of her passing.

When Jen was two years old, I had a dream she would die in her teens. I was so upset with this dream that I discussed it with someone I felt could help me with it. He thought perhaps the dream was speaking symbolically, referring to the stage when children enter their teens and begin to separate from the parents. But in my case the dream was not symbolic; it was premonitory.

Most often, death in a dream is meant to be interpreted symbolically, not literally. However, a small percentage of dreams may be prophetic. I think it is hard at the time of the dream to differentiate prophetic dreams from the normal "everyday" dreams. It is sometimes only in retrospect these prophetic dreams are discovered as being exactly that.

Another such example was a dream I had on October 17, 1992. In the dream, Jennifer was telling me she was going to continue dating a boy who I felt was not good for her. I said to her, "He kept bothering you to go back with him until you just couldn't say no, didn't he?"

She admitted that was the case. She was talking about marrying him. I was very upset, knowing it was not a good match, and she was making a mistake. I then saw her riding on a white horse, which was pulling a white carriage. I was panicked. I pulled her off the horse, and she fell to the ground. I thought she was dead. After a few minutes, she lifted her head and said, "I'm not really dead."

I was very upset when I awakened from the dream. I had no personal association with a white horse or white carriage, so I looked up "white horse" in a symbolic dictionary to determine its archetypal meaning. (Symbols in a dream can have a personal meaning, i.e., a meaning specific to the dreamer, or they may have a universal or archetypal meaning, one shared by a group of people or a specific culture.) In *A Dictionary of Symbols*, by J. E. Cirlot, it states: "In Germany and England, to dream of a white horse was thought to be an omen of death." My heritage is both German and English! I was very upset after reading that passage, and continued to be bothered by the dream. I never forgot it. The dream occurred three years (almost to the day) before Jennifer's death.

Six months before Jen died, I had another dream that may have been trying to prepare me. I have a "mother's ring" which contains a garnet—Jen's birthstone. Since she was an only child, I added my birthstone to the ring, as well as the diamond from my first marriage to give the ring more breadth. In this dream, I lost Jen's birthstone from that ring. In retrospect, this too, appeared to be an indication of what was to come.

After Jen's death, these dreams came flooding back to me. As I reread them and other dreams that seemed to be pointing toward losing her, I wondered if I should have been able to do something to prevent her death. I anguished over that for a long time. Later, I read in a book, whose title I can't recall at this point, that sometimes dreams like the ones I have described, are "given" to us to help prepare us at a subconscious level for a forthcoming trauma. The shock of losing a child brings us to our knees. There are some parents who don't survive it. Perhaps there was a part of me being prepared at some deep level.

I realized, since Jen watched me record my dreams several times a week while she was alive, she certainly would know after her passing she could reach me through dreams. And she continues to do just that. I cherish those visitation dreams. Almost every time I ask her to come to me in a dream she does.

She also comes at times that are particularly difficult for me. For example, I was a volunteer for the Big Brothers/Big Sisters organization, which is a mentoring program for children and teens. In the spring of 1997, I was paired with a "Little Sis," Jessica. Shortly after we were matched, she had a concert at her school where she would be singing a solo. She knew I did my own make-up for on-camera and stage work, and she asked if I would help her get ready for the concert. I agreed to, and when the evening came, I grabbed my Mary Kay kit and went over to her house. I helped Jessica with her make-up and she was off to the concert. I wasn't able to attend, since our dream group was meeting that evening. I held up well emotionally while with Jessica, but when I got in my car, I burst into tears. Helping a young teenage girl to apply make-up was too close to the heart. It reminded me of past times with Jennifer. I cried all the way to my meeting.

That night I dreamed the following:

> I heard the front doorbell ring. It was early morning and I was still sleeping. I got up to go to the door and Jen was standing in the living room, dressed in a white sweat suit. Her dark hair was pulled up in a pony tail and held in place by a white "scrunchie."

I was so glad to see her. She smiled at me, walked over to the front door, picked up a pink bottle of Mary Kay lotion, turned back to look at me, smiled again giving me a "thumbs-up," and walked out the door.

Later, in working with that dream, I realized Jen may have been trying to tell me she was pleased I helped Jessica with her make-up, even though it was difficult for me. I truly felt it was a visitation dream.

The women in the dream group bonded in a way like no other I have ever experienced. It has become very important for us to keep a connection with our children through dreams and through people like Anderson. It is helping us to survive the rest of this life without our children's physical presence.

–26–

Women in Military Service Memorial

Let us strive on to finish the work we are in; to bind up the nation's wounds; to care for him who shall have borne the battle, and for his widow, and his orphan—to do all which may achieve and cherish a just, and lasting peace, among ourselves, and with all nations.

~ Abraham Lincoln, The Second Inaugural Address

One spring evening, my friend and I decided to see a movie. I bought a newspaper to see what was currently playing. As I was waiting on hold to talk with her, I happened to glance down at the left side of the paper, opposite from the movie listings. A single line from Ann Landers's column, which was not highlighted in any way, caught my attention: "Women in Military Service Memorial."

In her column, Landers printed a letter from a man thanking her for writing about a Women's Military Memorial that was in the process of being built in Washington, D.C. She included the phone number of the memorial foundation for more information. I was so excited when I saw it—a memorial honoring women who served in the military! I seldom read the paper or watched the news, and the fact I came across this was quite synchronistic. I called the number right away and asked them to send me some information.

When the packet arrived, I pored through the contents. The memorial location would be at the gateway to Arlington National Cemetery. Inside the memorial, there was to be a "Memorial Register"—a computerized database with the name, photograph, and individual story of each woman's military service.

I thought it was a great way to honor the women who served in our military, and what a wonderful way for me to honor Jen. I filled out the application to enroll Jen as a charter member. I included her awards: Honor Graduate and Marksmanship Award, Parris Island. There was an area for each service woman to record memorable military experiences. I wasn't sure what to do there. Since Jen couldn't speak for herself, I thought about including a statement someone said about her.

I retrieved the folder of letters I received from Marine and Naval officials at the time of Jen's death. It was extremely difficult to read the letters again, and the tears flowed, as usual. I chose a quote from a letter by Admiral Prueher, Vice Chief of Naval Operations: "Jennifer's bright and energetic personality made a deep and lasting impression on us all, one I will not forget."

I called the memorial foundation to make sure it would be all right to use that. They said they thought it was a good idea. I completed the form, wrote the check for $25.00 and sent it along with her military picture. I felt like I was doing something concrete to help recognize Jennifer's efforts and contributions. I decided to attend the dedication in Washington on October 18.

I called Diane to see if she wanted to go with me. She was very excited about it. She remarked how, once again, we would be doing something special related to Jennifer around the time of the anniversary of her passing, as well as on Diane's birthday. Last year we were in New York; this year we would be in Washington D.C.

As excited as I was about attending the dedication, I was also extremely apprehensive about traveling to the place of my daughter's death. How would I react when I saw the Pentagon, and all the places that were a part of her life? What about seeing all those women in military uniforms? At this point in my life, every time I saw a young person in uniform in an airport or other public place, I would burst into tears. The Marines working at the *Toys for Tots* drop boxes were a prime example. I didn't know how I would do with all of that in Washington. There were already so many painful memories of Jen I encountered on a daily basis. Would I be adding insult to injury by traveling to Washington, or would it be a healing pilgrimage? At this point, I didn't know, but I had several months to prepare.

Around the same time I was making plans for the dedication, Gail and I were talking about taking a trip to France. Anna, one of the women we met on the Greece trip, was also interested, so we met to go over different tour packages. We decided on one that would include visits to several cities in France over the course of two weeks. I was hesitant about going, since I wasn't much fun to be around. But France sounded wonderful, so we set the dates for the end of August.

In early August, I was already beginning to feel the effects of the approaching second anniversary of Jen's passing. My sister Bobbi and my brother-in-law Mark had just celebrated their second wedding anniversary, which was a painful reminder of the last time I saw Jennifer.

The Sunday following their anniversary, I had a particularly difficult time at mass. For some reason, being in church frequently seemed to bring out the tears, and on this day they ran nonstop. A baby was going to be baptized after the mass, and Father made mention of that at the onset of the service. My tears began flowing, as I remembered the day Jen was baptized. I thought about the little white knitted dress and bonnet she wore, which I still have.

One of the readings that Sunday in August was a passage from 1 Kings 19: 1-8 about Elijah. The priest began to read that Elijah, after experiencing some very difficult times:

... went a day's journey into the desert, until he came to a broom tree and sat beneath it. He prayed for death: "This is enough, O Lord! Take my life, for I am no better than my fathers."

I barely dried my eyes and nose from seeing the baby in the baptismal outfit, when the tears flowed again, having heard the very words my own heart was crying out. I experienced enough pain and I was tired. I wanted to go "home" to Heaven. The priest went on to read:

He lay down and fell asleep under the broom tree, but then an angel touched him and ordered him to get up and eat. He looked and there at his head was a hearth cake and a jug of water. After he ate and drank, he lay down again, but the angel of the Lord came back a second time, touched him, and ordered, "Get up and eat, else the journey will be too long for you!" He got up, ate and drank; then strengthened by the food, he walked forty days and forty nights to the mountain of God, Horeb."

When mass was over, I left the church as quickly as I could. I cried all the way home and was still crying when the doorbell rang about fifteen minutes later. My cousin, Jim, and our mutual friend, Penny, were stopping by. I was very close to both of them and they certainly were aware of my pain.

I answered the door still crying and simply said as I waved them in, "I'm having a difficult day." We sat on the back porch and talked for a while. They listened to my pain as they so often had in the past. During the conversation, a cat walked across my deck. Penny asked if that was Kitty.

"No," I said, "but I would really like to see her again." Within seconds, another cat rounded the corner of the house. "That's her," I cried. "That's Kitty, at least I think it is. Let's see what she does."

She stopped and looked at us, then walked to where a statue of an angel representing Jen sat in my garden. Kitty lay down next to the statue and looked directly at us as if to say, "Now do you believe it's me?" I could hardly believe my eyes. Jim and Penny were in shock! It had been over a year since I had seen Kitty. I got my camera and took several pictures of her. I didn't think anyone would believe me if I told them what happened—even though there were three witnesses.

Kitty by Angel Statue

I guess God and Jen heard me crying under my own broom tree that day and sent Jim and Penny, as well as Kitty to give me strength and sustenance for my journey to Washington and the journey of my life without Jennifer. It's miracles like these that keep me going. I have a feeling Kitty will always be symbolic of that.

–27–

Arles, France

Sadness is but a wall between two gardens.

~ Kahlil Gibran, *Sand and Foam*

On August 23, Gail, Anna, and I left for France. We landed in Paris where we were to stay overnight before we began our tour through the countryside. We took a cruise down the Seine, saw the Eiffel Tower and the *Arc De Triomphe*. We would be coming back to Paris toward the end of our trip and would be able to spend a few more days there.

In the morning we began our journey through the country. Over the next few days, we stopped in the towns of Beaune, Lyon, Avignon, Monte Carlo, and Nice. France was absolutely beautiful and charming, but the pain of Jen's loss was a constant companion. I missed her so much. I would have loved for her to travel with me.

The evening after we left the South of France, I was lying in bed trying to fall asleep. I was "talking" to Jen in my head, asking her for a sign to let me know she was with me. For some reason, knowing for sure would make it easier.

In the morning when I awoke, I was disappointed she had not visited me in my dreams. But I hadn't specifically asked her for that. I merely requested a sign.

We loaded our luggage on the tour bus and continued our journey. As we traveled from town to town, the tour guide would point out the various sites. Sometimes I would pay attention, and sometimes my thoughts were elsewhere. I had not been listening closely at one point when his voice drifted back into my awareness. He was saying something about wanting to take a short detour to Arles. He said he realized it was not on our itinerary, but there was a bridge a famous artist had used in one of his paintings, and he was interested in seeing it again. He explained the bridge had been undergoing renovation, and he hadn't seen it in over a year. He wanted to see the progress and asked if we were interested in stopping there.

I leaned over to Anna and asked who the painter was.

"Vincent Van Gogh," she replied.

I burst into tears. I asked for a sign from Jen the evening before, and the next day the tour bus takes a detour and goes to the city where Van Gogh lived for approximately a year. I couldn't contain myself.

Seeing my reaction, Anna asked what was wrong. I told her how I associated Jen's death with the song "Vincent" and how I had asked Jen for a sign just the night before. I was crying so hard I had to put on my sunglasses when we got off the bus to see the bridge.

Isn't that just like my Marine daughter to "hijack" an entire tour bus because Mom wanted a sign? I was moved beyond words. I must have taken a dozen pictures of the Langlois Bridge where Van Gogh painted the bridge with a horse and buggy crossing and women washing their clothing in the water below.

The Langlois Bridge at Arles, France, Painting by Vincent Van Gogh

Photo by Joyce Harvey

The Langlois Drawbridge at Arles, France

As the days progressed, we saw many beautiful sites. The day we were in Bordeaux, we learned Princess Diana of Whales died in an auto accident in Paris. We were stunned, as was the rest of the world. What made it even more surreal is we would be back in Paris in a few days. Thousands were mourning her death. I felt for one moment in time, the world and I were on the same page—that of profound grief.

On our way back to Paris, we stopped in Normandy. Seeing the white grave markers at the American Cemetery was very moving. It struck me for each grave, there were loved ones left behind to grieve. As we were walking back to the tour bus, "Taps" was played. The mournful notes of the melody transported me back to the day of Jen's funeral. Once again, the tears fell. The people on the tour with me must have wondered who this woman was who was crying so often. By now, I was used to the tears. They had become a way of life.

We visited Rouen, where Joan of Arc was burned at the stake. I felt drawn to the actual site where she died, and the nearby church built in her honor. I thought of how she is such a role model for courage—especially for those who are called to walk a path few seem to understand.

Returning to Paris was quite sobering—seeing the flowers at the accident site and watching the BBC broadcasts of Princess Diana's life. My heart went out to her young sons and to the rest of her family as well. Their lives would forever be changed. I knew that only too well.

–28–

"You're on the Right Path"

Carefully observe what way your heart draws you,
and then choose that way with all your strength.

~ Hasidic Saying

Shortly following my return from France, I was to lead a large training initiative preparing the Ford Motor Company models and narrators for the auto show, which debuted in January. Having once been an auto show narrator for Ford, coupled with my experience of product training gave me the necessary background. The program, which was three days in length and involving approximately 75 people, would prepare the participants for the shows that would take place throughout the country over the next eight months. I taught this program for the past five years, but I wasn't sure if I should take on the project again this year. I hadn't been as involved with the technical aspects of the material as I once was, so it would take an enormous amount of time and effort to get up to speed with the changes that occurred in the industry within the past year. I wasn't sure I had that kind of energy. In addition, the program took place at the end of September, right as I was heading into the second anniversary of Jen's passing. After much deliberation I made the decision to do the training for one more year.

A few days before the training was to begin, I was talking with my cousin, Jim. He has always been a good sounding board for me and at the same time, is able to help me decipher the guidance my dreams seemed to be giving me. I had been thinking about making some considerable changes with regard to my career. In addition, I was entertaining thoughts of writing a book about losing Jen and sharing with others the awareness that our loved ones continue to exist in spirit form.

I had actually begun the writing, but to devote the amount of time and energy needed, I would have to cut back dramatically on my work schedule. To walk away from a good income and career to write the book was a real leap of faith for me. My dreams were guiding me in this direction, but like most people, I wanted a *big* sign. I remember discussing this with my cousin Jim saying, "Where is Edgar Cayce when you need him?" Cayce, who was born in the late 1800's and who was known as the "Sleeping Prophet" would give "readings" to people by going into a trance-like sleep. I longed for that type of guidance at this juncture in my life. "I wish," I continued talking with Jim, "that someone would walk up to me and tell me I'm on the right path!"

The training project was at hand, and the first two days went well. I bonded with the participants over the years and we were always glad to see each other. They had great respect for me and for my knowledge base. The compliments poured forth, and I felt I had made the right decision to do the project one last time. It's almost as if they knew the questions in my heart, which of course, they didn't.

At the end of the second day, we all gathered for dinner at an exclusive restaurant. We were given a separate banquet room solely for our use. I sat down next to a wonderful woman, Susan, who lived in California. She knew this was a difficult time of year for me. Jen died just a week or so after we finished this same training in 1995.

All of the participants had been informed, and they sent flowers, plants, cards, and prayers. Susan asked how I was doing, and I told her each day was a struggle. She nodded and began to share with me that when she was in her teens, she lost a sister, and it was very difficult for her. We continued our intense conversation as we got up to go to the salad bar. Ahead of me in line was a young man by the name of Leo. This was his second year in the program and I didn't know him very well. He struck up a conversation with us and began to ask the usual social questions. He asked me if I had any children. Once again, I felt the knife-like pain in my heart that always accompanies such a question. I took a breath and told him I had one daughter who died two years ago.

He looked directly at me and said, "She's still with you."

"I know," I responded.

He proceeded to share with Susan and me that not long ago he lost his sister, Brenda. This was turning into an extraordinary conversation in a most unusual setting. I invited Leo to join us at our table, which he did. Everyone else was partying and having a good time, in contrast to the three of us with our heads together in a tearful, intense conversation.

Leo talked about his sister and shared they had some differences between them right before her death. He said he struggled with that for some time.

In the middle of his story, he looked at me and said, totally out of context, "You know you're on the right path." Without missing a beat, he proceeded with his story about Brenda. I was stunned. Just a day or two prior, I had been talking with Jim about wanting a sign indicating I was heading down the right road!

One other time in the course of the evening, and again on the third day of training, Leo said to me (out of the blue) "You're on the right path." He had no idea of my conversation with Jim or of little else in my life.

Leo also shared with us he had been at a meeting, where he was approached by a woman named Lisa, whom he had never met before.

She said to Leo, "I normally don't do this sort of thing, but I have to ask you, do you know a Brenda?"

Leo nodded.

Lisa said, "I have a message from Brenda. She wants you to know she is all right, and she holds nothing against you. She wants you to be at peace with that."

Leo told us he tearfully admitted to Lisa that Brenda was his deceased sister.

Susan and I listened with amazement. Leo wrote down Lisa's phone number and encouraged me to get in touch with her.

If I hadn't taught this workshop one more time, I never would have found out about Lisa.

A few days later when I called Leo to thank him for his referral, I said to him, "I have to tell you something." I described my earlier conversation with Jim, asking God for a sign I was on the right path. "Do you realize, Leo, that three times in the course of our conversations, you told me I was on the right path?"

He shared with me that when I first told him I lost a child, he immediately prayed, asking God, "If there is any way I can be of help to this woman, please use me as a vehicle."

I was astounded with what I just heard. He certainly had been of enormous help—passing on the message I was on the right path and telling me about Lisa. What a selfless, unconditional act of love and service.

–29–

Further Proof the Spirit Survives

*Grant that I may seek not so much
to be consoled as to console.*

~ Prayer of St. Francis of Assisi

I called Lisa to schedule an appointment. Leo explained she only does "readings" if she gets a personal referral from someone she knows. I didn't tell her anything about myself except that Leo referred me. She agreed to see me and told me she had an opening on October 3—a day after the second anniversary of Jen's passing! I told her that would work for me, and she gave me directions to her place. I didn't tell anyone I was going to see her.

On October 2, I attended a mass for Jen and took flowers to her grave. I spent the evening with the women in my dream group. I wasn't sure if I could even go out that day, but I felt if anyone would understand the difficult time I was having, it would be my friends who were also bereaved mothers.

I shared with them that in a few days, I would be attending a convention in Chicago, where one of the speakers would be James Van Praagh. Like Anderson, Van Praagh also has the ability to pass messages on from the spirit world. He will often do random readings at his seminars, passing on messages from loved ones on "the other side."

Regina wanted to go with me to Chicago, but she wasn't able to. She told me she had been praying to God for a sign from Mark, and also "talking" to Mark, asking him to get a message through me if possible. At this point, Regina did not know I was going to see Lisa the next day.

The following day, when I arrived at Lisa's apartment, she and I bonded immediately. I found her to be a vibrant and compassionate individual. I had a good feeling about her right from the start. She shared with me she had survived two episodes of kidney cancer and also had a near-death experience.

I didn't share anything about me and after handing me a glass of water, she began the reading. "There is a young woman here who has a number of animals with her. She looks like Dr. Doolittle."

She described a colorful bird on Jen's shoulder, as well as other animals she had surrounding her. That was certainly consistent with Jen's life-long love of animals and with Anderson's message about Jen working with animals on the other side. What struck me even further is that I have a picture of Jen taken at Busch Gardens in Tampa when she was approximately six or seven. She has a live toucan sitting on her shoulder.

At one point, after she established Jen's name, Lisa said, "Jen wants to know if you're going to pass out candy this year at Halloween."

"I don't know," I replied.

"She wants to know if you're going to dress up," Lisa asked.

Every fall for a number of years, I performed in a musical play with a local community theater group. Each Halloween I dressed up in my current costume from the play and passed out candy. One year it was Annie Oakley, the next year Mammy Yokum, from *Little Abner*. One of the last roles I played was that of Snow White. I had a very authentic costume that was made for me, complete with the red bow for my dark hair. I remember the first time I saw myself in full costume. I looked so much like Snow White it was shocking. I bought the costume from the theater group upon completion of the play. Every Halloween following the play I dressed up as Snow White to pass out candy.

I played "dumb" and asked Lisa, "What does Jen think I should dress up as?"

Lisa paused for a moment and said, "I'm hearing a Disney song." She then looked at me and said, "Oh, Snow White!"

I almost fell off my chair. Lisa went on to say, "Jen put a red bow in your hair and said, 'Well, who do you think she looks like?' There was no doubt in my mind Lisa was absolutely transmitting messages from my daughter.

Lisa asked me, "Do you know a Mark?"

"Yes."

"Jen sees Mark all the time."

Jen said (through Lisa), "Mom, Mark is very good at what he does over here. He works with children. He helps them cross over."

Once again, I was speechless. I remembered what Regina shared with me regarding Mark's visit in her niece's dream. There was no way Lisa could have known this. It also struck me profoundly Regina had specifically asked Mark to get a sign through me. She did not know I was going to see Lisa.

Lisa went on to share other information with me from Jen and from one of my guides. The entire reading was extremely accurate. I asked Jen once again, if my talking to her kept her from doing what she needed to do on the other side.

"Not at all," she replied. Jen explained the spirit world is not as finite as ours, nor do they experience time the same way we do.

I came away from the reading feeling a sense of peace and joy at having connected with her once again. I was reassured once more she was still with me.

When I got in my car to return home, I called Regina from my cellular phone. I told her I had been to see a medium and that Mark came through. I asked her if she wanted to hear the tape.

She said "Absolutely. Can you come straight here?"

Within two hours Regina, Mounir, and I were listening to Jen's message. Needless to say, Regina and Mounir were overwhelmed by what they heard on the tape. It was an affirmation of what their niece had learned in the dream. It was also an affirmation that our loved ones hear our prayers, our thoughts, and our requests. The reading with Lisa brought more peace, healing, and confirmation into our lives.

-30-

Pilgrimage to Washington, D.C.

Although the world is full of suffering,
it is also full of the overcoming of it.

~ Helen Keller

The Women in Military Service Memorial dedication, scheduled for October 18, 1997 was fast approaching. When I awoke on the morning of October 9, I recorded the following dream:

> We moved Jen's body to a new cemetery. We had her flag-draped casket on rollers. Other people, friends, were with me; they were all women. We were pushing the casket across a parking lot.
>
> There was another funeral taking place. It was a military funeral, except it wasn't one of the four branches of the military. The soldiers, many of whom were women, were dressed in red uniforms. The person who died was a young woman, eighteen or nineteen years of age who committed suicide. Their ceremony was

finishing up. We walked past her casket, which was open. I didn't look in. It reminded me too much of Jen's funeral. They began to move her coffin toward the burial place. This ceremony seemed to be taking place in a parking lot outside. It was a nice day.

We tried to move a little faster with Jen's casket so we wouldn't get behind this other funeral procession, but they eventually moved ahead of us.

We had to pass through an area where we were required to buy a ticket. We paid our money. Someone reminded me I could use my employee pass to get through. I showed it to the person taking the money. She refunded our money and let us through.

My friends went ahead with Jen's casket and left it at the burial site. I hoped the cemetery caretaker got it buried in the right place. I wouldn't be able to see Jen's grave as much now that it was moved.

At the time I had the dream, I didn't tie it in with the approaching dedication in Washington. But I was soon to see aspects of my dream flash before my eyes.

I wanted to participate in the entire weekend of events in Washington, which consisted of a formal dinner Thursday evening called the "Gala," the actual dedication of the memorial on Saturday, and a candlelight march and service Saturday evening honoring deceased military. Diane had a friend living in Arlington who invited us to stay with her. We took her up on the offer.

When we arrived in Washington, my concerns about the pilgrimage soon began to fade. Instead of feeling anxious or sad, I felt a sense of peace and excitement. We put on our evening dresses for the Gala and took a taxi to the event. When we arrived, I saw a number of young women in military uniforms assisting the guests. I wondered if Jen would have been working at this event if she were still alive. It was incredible to see women of all ages, dressed in formal attire, gathered by the hundreds.

The Gala event was wonderful. We sat at a table with four other people, including a Marine who served in the Pacific during World War II. We had a wonderful dinner and enjoyed presentations by Tipper Gore, and actresses Connie Stevens, Nancy Giles, and Loretta Swit. Following dinner there was a concert by Kathy Mattea. It was a memorable evening and a great way to begin the weekend festivities.

On Friday, the various branches of the military were having reunions. Since Diane and I weren't involved with those, we toured D.C. We visited some of the Smithsonian Institution museums and all of the monuments: The Washington Monument, Lincoln Memorial, the Vietnam Veterans Memorial, and the Korean War Veterans Memorial. Soon, there would be one more added to the roster. We would be part of that historical moment.

On the morning of the dedication, Diane's friend dropped us off at the site so we wouldn't have to deal with parking. Thousands of chairs were set up in the parking lot in front of Arlington National Cemetery. There were large screens by the dais so those in the back could see the events. There was an impressive array of guests on the dais: Vice President and Mrs. Gore, Supreme Court Judge Sandra Day O'Connor, Secretary of Defense William Cohen, and General Colin Powell, just to name a few.

Kenny Rogers and Patti Austin sang a beautiful song written specifically for the dedication, "I Will Always Remember You." As the procession of flags of the states and territories began, I was stunned to see it being led by personnel representing the Revolutionary War wearing red military uniforms. My dream of the military funeral flashed before my eyes—the red coats! The dream setting was a parking lot in front of a cemetery. That is exactly where we were at the moment—on the parking lot in front of Arlington National Cemetery.

In addition, the members of the Marine Corps band were wearing red coats. The dream gave me details I had not known before my arrival in Washington. I thought about the dream's symbolism of Jen being interned, so to speak, at Arlington. Inside the memorial, which we had yet to see, would be Jen's picture and information in a database. I nudged Diane wide-eyed and told her about my dream.

We were caught up in the excitement of this historic moment. I was wearing Jen's military shoes so she could "walk with me." I found it very profound to be among all those women who served our country over the years, from as far back as World War I, to women who are currently serving. I watched Vietnam veterans embrace who hadn't seen each other in over twenty years. Many of the women wore their military uniforms. They journeyed from all parts of the country. I felt like saying "Thank you," to each and every one of them. "Thank you for serving our country."

During the ceremony, a new *Women in Military Service* postage stamp was unveiled, representing the five branches of the military (including the Coast Guard). Diane and I had our picture taken next to the large display of the stamp following the ceremony.

In the evening, a candlelight vigil was held. Approximately 15,000 people gathered according to their individual branch of the military, in an area across from the Lincoln Memorial. Diane and I stood with the Marines. Each of us was given a battery-operated candle, like one would see in windows at Christmas. A military band was playing as each group began to fall in line. All traffic was stopped as we marched across the bridge over the Potomac to the Memorial at Arlington National Cemetery. It was an extraordinary experience. There was such unity and synergy. Frequently the women's voices could be heard singing the hymn of the Marine Corps, or of their respective branch of the service.

At one point, I turned and looked back upon thousands of candles waving in the air, set against the backdrop of an illuminated Lincoln Memorial. It is a moment that will always remain with me. I felt such love and peace marching with these women. Maybe I had to do this to heal the wounds in my heart inflicted by a small number of military personnel.

As we all reached the site of the memorial and took our seats, a service was held for those military personnel no longer with us. A representative from each branch gave a tribute to their deceased comrades. The last two people to speak were parents who lost children while serving in the military. They spoke for me and for everyone who loaned a child to our country, only to never have them come home again. As they completed their tribute, they took some rose petals and threw them in the reflecting pool in front of the memorial.

At the conclusion of the ceremony, thousands of voices began to sing, "Let there be peace on earth, and let it begin with me," each voice paired with a candle moving in synchrony with the music. Upon the final note of the song, we turned to see a beautiful fireworks display over the Potomac. As I reflected on the words of the song, I knew somehow, I would have to find peace in my heart, to truly put my pain and anguish to rest. Maybe that's what the dream was trying to tell me—that coming here would be an opportunity to lay it all to rest. In many ways, this pilgrimage to Washington had brought me some peace, some closure. But there was still one more thing I had to do.

I walked up to the reflecting pool and threw some rose petals in for Jennifer. Diane and I went inside the memorial, to a room housing the Memorial Registry. I wrote Jen's name on a piece of paper and handed it to an attendant, who pulled up the appropriate screen on the computer. There was my beautiful daughter in her Marine Dress Blues. I stood there looking at the screen with tears running freely, as I whispered to her, "I'm proud of you, Jen, and I love you." I felt in a small way, I helped to ensure the memory of my daughter's service to this country, no matter how short-lived, would not be forgotten.

The Monday after I arrived home, I bought some of the *Women in Military* stamps at the post office. Every time I used one, I drew a little heart under the picture of the Marine, my Marine. I guess it represented the piece of my heart left in Washington. I will never forget being a part of that historic moment—not only for the country, but in my own healing journey as well.

–31–

Starry, Starry Night in Arles

He who has a why to live for can bear almost any how.

~ Friedrich Nietzche

In November, Meredith spent a weekend with me. It had been a while since we had seen each other, and it was great to connect again. I shared the George Anderson reading with her the last time we were together, and filled her in on the extraordinary "side" trip to Arles, France.

At one point during her visit, she was looking through a book I have on the artwork of Andy Lakey. The book tells his incredible story of going from a drug-abusing car salesman to a celebrated artist. The transformation took place when he had a near-death experience, during which he saw seven angels. After his recovery, he began to sketch the angels he saw. Several years later, he was visited again by three angels who inspired him to create two thousand angel paintings by the year 2000.

Meredith was mesmerized by his story. Lakey had never painted before his NDE, and yet he was now world famous. Equally as impressive, were the inspirational stories from the collectors of Andy's work. I asked her if she would like her own copy of the book as my Christmas gift to her. Her eyes lit up immediately. I suggested we go to a local bookstore to see if we could find it. I purchased mine at the same gallery where I acquired one of Lakey's 2000 series paintings, so I wasn't sure if we could find it in a bookstore.

At the store we looked in the inspirational and spiritual sections but didn't find it there. Meredith suggested we look under the art section. There I found a copy of a large pictorial account of Vincent van Gogh's work.

I pulled it off the shelf and said to Meredith, "I want to show you what 'The Starry Night' looks like." I turned to that page. On the right side of the book was the picture, and on the left side, a description and narrative. I sucked in my breath as I read Van Gogh had painted *two* versions of "The Starry Night," the first of which he painted in Arles, France! I never knew there were two versions. My daughter had "taken" me to the city where the original version of "The Starry Night" was painted.

Meredith and I looked at each other speechless. As we began to recover from our shock, she announced she was getting this book for me for Christmas. It was not a cheap book, and it was really more than she should be spending on me. She insisted.

As we walked toward the cashier, I suggested we look at the bargain book section, as I normally do whenever I'm in the store. There to my surprise was a different picture book featuring Van Gogh's work, marked down to half price. It was every bit as beautiful as the one in our hands. I quickly leafed through it to find if it contained the Arles version of "The Starry Night!" It was the only copy among the bargain books. Meredith bought that one for me instead.

We were so profoundly moved by what we had discovered, we drove home in silence. We never did find the Lakey book, but what we found was a gift beyond description.

I wondered what it all meant. How are our loved ones able to guide us from the other side, helping us to find evidence they are still with us? How does one explain something like this? I don't know.

What I do know is when these experiences happen to you over and over again, there's no denying them. The bond between Jennifer and me was so strong in life she could read my thoughts. Is it any wonder the bond continues to be strong even after her death? Messages via tour guides, dreams, songs, books, and kittens—I have a feeling this journey will continue for me, and for anyone who remains open to the possibilities.

–32–

Lessons from the Swans

*The swan is the quintessential symbol of transformation,
a living montage of that which was perceived as ugly or
awkward to that which is recognized for its grace, substance,
and beauty. The swan is also symbolic of the soul and soul
growth, often not recognizable unless a "mirror"
is provided to reflect the transformation.*

~ Joyce Harvey

The years following Jennifer's death have been agonizing and confusing. I am slowly climbing out of the abyss and beginning to collect the pieces of my shattered world. Some of the pieces are gone forever; some don't seem to fit any more; and there are new pieces I have found, and will continually find along the way.

I suppose it's like any explosion that goes deep enough—one may find diamonds and gems amidst the rubble, since they are often buried deep inside. It takes time, strength, and courage to sort through the rubble—to take a close look at each and every piece, choosing what you will glue into the new mosaic pattern of your life, and what truly doesn't belong.

I will never be the same, but with time and healing, one creates a new normal. I just don't know what that new normal will be. Periodically, I look at my own reflection in the water to see how the mosaic is evolving. I strongly sense each of us has a purpose for being on this earth. That is why we remain here, even though someone we dearly love has crossed over. It is not yet our time to go.

I can already feel the pull in new directions. Jen's death wasn't the only death I experienced. As a result of her passing, there are aspects of myself that have died—some that needed to die. I don't get upset at the small things in life anymore. It's easier to keep my priorities straight. I don't lose sight of the "bigger picture" as often as I used to. I can stand up to bullies, regardless of their status, with deep conviction and less fear. After all, they can't hurt me any more than I've already been hurt.

Maybe one of the lessons we need to master when going through tragedy is to emerge on the other side of it without having taken on the "ugly duckling" traits of bitterness, anger, and self-pity. That is no easy task.

Hopefully, we come to understand that deep in our souls we are all beautiful swans. It is this "swan spirit" that continues to live on. It's an incredible gift if we can connect with it, not only within ourselves, but also with our loved ones on the physical plane and those who continue to exist in spirit. But just as the ugly duckling was blind to his true being until he saw his reflection, we can't know this truth unless we are willing to look for it. It takes courage to face the traumas, losses, and dark sides in our lives.

Perhaps we can learn a lesson from a flock of swans that had flown south one winter, thinking they would escape the forthcoming cold, only to end up covered with snow. The swans stood facing directly into the fierce winter wind, because to turn away would allow the frigid air to get under their feathers, and they would freeze to death.

Sometimes, the only way to truly survive the bitterly cold winter of grief is to face it head on … and then … to hang on, trusting in our hearts that spring must surely come again.

The End

Endnotes

1 "Vincent," Don McLean, p. 26.
2 Raymond Moody, Jr., M.D., *The Light Beyond* (New York: Bantam Books, 1988), p. 95.
3 "One Day More!," Les Misérables, p. 115.
4 "One Day More!," Les Misérables, p. 122.

Notes

Notes

About the Author

Joyce Harvey

Joyce Harvey is an inspirational speaker and writer. She is also the author of *I'm Fine ... I'm With the Angels*, an illustrated children's book on dying and life after death, and the author of *How Do You Grow a New Heart?* She is a contributing author for *Chicken Soup for the Unsinkable Soul*, *Chicken Soup for the Grieving Soul*, and *Chicken Soup for the Recovering Soul: Daily Inspirations*.

Ms. Harvey is active in the national and local bereavement community. She has spoken at a number of grief conferences, including The Compassionate Friends, Alive Alone, and The International Conference on Bereavement.

Joyce was selected as an "Outstanding Young Woman of America" for her professional achievements and her contribution to the community. She has a background in nursing and taught critical care nursing courses to RNs who worked in critical care units.

Jennifer was her only child.

Joyce can be reached at: info@joyceanneharvey.com.

For more information visit her website at: www.joyceanneharvey.com.